In All Your Getting, Get Understanding!

A Handbook for Your Life Journey

By

Pastor Dennis Scott

In All Your Getting, Get Understanding! A Handbook for Your Life Journey

By Dennis Scott

ISBN:0692969209

ISBN:9780692969205

Dedication

This handbook is dedicated to every believer, unbeliever, and to those who are incarcerated. I dedicate this handbook to parents, single parents, single individuals, and husbands and wives of all nationalities on every economic level of life. I dedicate this handbook to military service members (active and retired), and to civilians all around the world. Moreover, I dedicate this handbook to anyone who seeks to understand life on Earth with God — as we all journey along the way.

Acknowledgments

I offer up praises of thanksgiving to my Heavenly Father. Through the Holy Spirit, He has placed in me, gifts for His glory and empowered me to write this Handbook. I thank Him because He continues to strengthen me.

To my lovely wife, Janelle, a woman that God specifically designed for, gifted and blessed me with, I thank you for all you do for our household, and for all you do, on purpose, for me. You are absolutely beautiful, and a marvelous partner to have in marriage. You are a part of my shared vision, and I thank you for helping me to make this handbook a reality — a dream and a goal, accomplished.

To the best team, my beloved children — all-grown-up — that a father could have: Cebronica, Jamye, Jamal, and my granddaughter, Na'Ja, I thank you for your love and support. Thank you for showering me with your unconditional love. You guys are the best! Thank you for putting up with me.

To my mom, Ruth, and to my sister, Cynthia, I thank God for you both. Mother, thank you for your years of sacrifice. You worked overtime on a regular basis to see that we got whatever we needed, and as many of our desires that we wanted. And you ensured that we knew God. Cynthia, you are precious and a strong woman of God. I am blessed to have you for a sister.

I want to thank Dr. Michael Freeman, senior pastor of *Spirit of Faith Christian Center* (SOFCC) in Temple Hills, MD, and First Lady Dr. Dee Dee Freeman. You guys are the best! I thank God for the both of you, stirring up the gifts in me.

To my Prison Ministry team, at *Spirit of Faith Christian Center*, you all are great and caring. I am grateful to be in partnership with you, serving men and women in jails and prisons.

I am grateful to all the overseas chaplains, those pastors and ministers, I served with in Sasebo and Yokosuka Japan, and Pastor Sam Rachal Jr., in Bremerton, Washington. You all added increase that pushed me ahead, shaped my life and helped me learn about what it means to be a minister, a man of God, a husband, a father and a friend.

I want to express my appreciation to an excellent editor, Yvonne J. Medley. Our weeks and months side-by-side with the Holy Spirit's help has been absolutely remarkable. You are a valuable treasure, a woman of God for all to see and know. Thank you for allowing the Holy Spirit to use you to help me put this handbook together as a vehicle that will be in the hands of readers for God's glory.

My expression of gratitude would not be complete without giving tribute to my aunts, uncles, cousins, nieces, nephews, in-laws, and dear friends (including those who have gone on to glory). I want to express my gratitude to my in-laws, the late Margaret and Gerald Cain; to my childhood friends from Randolph Avenue in New Jersey; my military friends, and to every church denomination family of which I have been blessed to be a part. I am grateful for each of you. In many ways, you all have added increase to my life — from childhood to this present day. I thank you.

Introduction

Welcome! Together we are embarking on a level of understanding that may have been hard for most of us to get, alone.

I could not understand why my life was not changing based on what I had heard church people say. And whenever trouble arose, their mantra was always, "God will fix it!" But I needed to know more. I needed to know how and when, and what — if anything — I needed to do to place myself on the path *to be fixed.*

Moreover, I thought that once I had been saved that all my problems would vanish. It was not so. Disappointment and confusion caused me to devise my own shortcuts and temporary fixes. I spent my years faltering in circles like the Israelites who were bound in circles of the wilderness. Not understanding God, and therefore not obeying God, bewildered my life experiences. It was like I just couldn't get a break. I felt that I knew God. I felt that I was calling out to God. But He just couldn't hear me. Why? Through this period in my life, I had failed to understand that God wanted to provide escape routes to my circles. He wanted to lead me to Him, and to a better life. Seeking godly understanding about faith, renewing my mind, casting down negative thoughts, and more, changed my life's course.

God wants us to experience what the Word says, to do what the Word says, and to be what the Word says.

During my early walk with God, I did not understand the power of the Holy Spirit living in me — plain and simple. And that is why sharing *In All Your Getting, Get Understanding!* means so much to me. Beloved, after you have read it, I pray that it will mean much to you as well.

Preface

Concerning Proverbs 4:7 (NKJV), "Wisdom is the principal thing; Therefore get wisdom. And in all your getting, get understanding." This has settled in my spirit — to seek God, believe and to allow the Holy Spirit to guide me in writing this handbook. The information found *In All Your Getting, Get Understanding!* will help new Christians as well as the unsaved. Many born-again Christians fail to understand the next steps needed after receiving Jesus as Lord and Savior. For many, they may find themselves in churches that are not properly teaching the Word of God. For others, they may not have even joined a church, yet.

You may ask yourself, how do I, the author of this handbook, know this? It's because years ago, I was one of those born-again Christians in the bunch, finding myself succumbed to a lack of understanding. During my twenty-four years in the United States Navy, I traveled around the world, and while doing so, I participated in different church denominations in search of the Word of God. I knew that I needed to connect myself with a body of believers in order to walk my newly-found walk, effectively. And what I discovered was that each church denomination I came upon had its own religious traditions, interpretations of the Word, and sometimes, they even harbored distinct ways of how to live for God. Suddenly, it seemed to me that their religious traditions were more important than teaching the Word of truth. Check this, Colossians 2:8 (NKJV) says, "Beware lest anyone cheat you through philosophy and empty deceit, according to the tradition of men, according to the basic principles of the world, and not according to Christ."

Please do not get me wrong, regarding religious tradition. I'm not saying that church/denominational traditions are not important to the order of things, or that they are not, perhaps, needed. What I am saying is that they should not override the importance of teaching what the Word of God says. For years, I came across loving people of God, standing in the position to teach, but they were not versed in the Word of God. Such mishap caused me years of unsolved challenges, issues and frustration, and it pitted me in the land of the unknown. What I longed for was a clear understanding, and to be a doer, as found in James 1:22 (NKJV), of God's Word by faith.

Now, considering the Word, I am not blaming anyone for my lack of knowledge. Hosea 4:6 (NKJV) says, "My people are destroyed for lack of knowledge. Because you have rejected knowledge, I also will reject you from being priest for Me; Because you have forgotten the law of your God, I also will forget your children." Check this out: the children of Israel not only had a lack of knowledge, but also they had rejected or forgotten knowledge (God's Law/Word) as well. I have a responsibility, like everyone else, to seek out and apply what I've learned from the Word of God. Those who prayerfully taught me, and others, did their best based on what was taught to them. I thank God for now knowing the truth about Him and His Word as well as the tools He placed in my path — for just such a discovery. Learning and living the true Word of God set me free from those unsolved challenges, issues and frustrations, according to John 8:32.

Have you ever been frustrated about something that you just didn't understand? Is there a current challenge that continues to prevent you from receiving sweet sleep (Proverbs 3:24) — the sweet sleep you should receive because you are now a child of God? Perhaps the reason for your frustration is rooted in your lack of understanding about the challenges you're facing.

Your frustration will only mount without a clear understanding of how to positively proceed through any challenge and/or negative issue. Because of your frustration, you may find yourself moving further away from God, not closer via fellowship with the Holy Spirit. This happens especially when there is no one around to help you.

Another reason for this handbook's purpose is to reinforce your life journey with God. This handbook is also designed to help provide an understanding about what it means to live with the Holy Spirit inside you, especially as He moves you toward your providence.

Another important factor is wisdom. Wisdom is a principal part of our lives as believers. It allows any believer to apply God-given resources and solutions to any one of our life challenges. For example, Word knowledge teaches us to forgive and to love everyone. Wisdom teaches us to obey that Word knowledge; and understanding teaches us how to activate and maintain that Word knowledge. Having wisdom is the principal foundation.

Experiencing In All Your Getting, Get Understanding! I believe, will add a boost to your life, while learning how to live with and trust the Holy Spirit. It will guide you on the next life-giving steps after you receive Jesus as your Lord and Savior. Moreover, this handbook will give those, who have been walking with God, a new awareness of the Holy Spirit's power that is at work in their lives. It will assist you in the pursuit of your dreams, goals and the godly desires of your heart — on Earth.

Table of Contents

CHAPTER ONE — Let Us Get Started

God wants everyone to be saved.

In 1 Timothy 2:3-4 (NKJV), it says, "For this is good and acceptable in the sight of God our Savior, who desires all men [people] to be saved and to come to the knowledge of the truth."

First let's be clear, if you are among the unsaved, meaning that you're either sitting on the fence or otherwise, here's your opportunity to change the direction of your life. Nothing is by accident. God wants you to know He loves you, and He wants you to accept His only begotten Son, Jesus, for salvation.

Let me share something that you may be hearing for the first time. Without a clear understanding of God's blessings, the raw truth could be upsetting to you. It might even cause you to close your heart, and thereby miss out on information that is vital for you, right now. Please pause and relax to objectively consume this next very real statement: Everyone is created by God, but not everyone is a child of God. Again, relax, it's going to be all right. You are on your way to getting understanding.

Secondly, stay focused, and let me explain. For someone to say that he or she attends church, or does well in life by helping others — such good deeds do not determine salvation. Let's say that such a person also doesn't drink, smoke, or steal, but instead works to do everything that he or she defines what a good person should be; none of those attributes determines salvation. Such an on-purpose lifestyle can erroneously lead a person to believe that he or she is a child of God.

As awful as it may sound, about not being a child of God, it is the truth, based on the Bible. If you are possibly turned off by what you've prayerfully learned thus far, I promise you that God loves you. In John 8:32 (NASB), it says, "… and you will know the truth, and the truth will make you free." That's what you want to know, the truth regarding everything in life on Earth, especially, when it concerns you.

Additionally, here's a bit more on the subject to get a better understanding from the Bible. Here is what the Bible says, according to John 3:16 (NKJV), "For God so loved the world that He gave His only begotten Son, that whoever believes in Him should not perish but have everlasting life." Everyone is God's creation — according to Colossians 1:16 (NKJV), "For by Him [God] all things were created that are in heaven and that are on Earth, visible and invisible, whether thrones or dominions or principalities or powers. All things were created through Him and for Him."

Let's take in the difference between being God's creation and being a child of God. According to John 1:11-12 (NKJV) it says, "He [Jesus] came to His own, and His own did not receive Him. But as many as received Him, to them He gave the right to become children of God, to those who believe in His name." Now did you get that? The Bible says that to anyone who receives Jesus, He has given that person the right to become a child of God.

Let me say it this way, if anyone receives Jesus Christ into his or her life as Lord and Savior, Christ gives to him or her right to be called a child of God. This is regardless of class, race, nationality, or economic status or power. Also know that there is neither an amount of good deeds nor amount of money, rendered that will clear a pathway to becoming a child of God. The only pathway, according to the Bible, is by accepting Jesus Christ as your Lord and Savior (Romans 10: 9-10).

Let's move on —

Romans 8:9 (NKJV) says toward the end of that verse, "Now if anyone does not have the Spirit of Christ, he [or she] is not His."

Romans 8:16 (NKJV) says, “The Spirit Himself bears witness with our spirit that we are children of God.” This means that because we are a spirit that lives in our bodies, the Holy Spirit bears witness of our spirit. This happens by accepting Jesus Christ as Lord and Savior. Romans10:9 (NKJV) says, “… that if you confess with your mouth the Lord Jesus and believe in your heart that God has raised Him from the dead, you will be saved.” You will see this confession as you read more.

1 John 3:1-2 (NKJV) says, “Behold what manner of love the Father has bestowed on us, that we should be called children of God! Therefore, the world does not know us, because it did not know Him. Beloved, now we are children of God; and it has not yet been revealed what we shall be, but we know that when He is revealed, we shall be like Him for we shall see Him as He is.”

Let’s move on —

Here is what you should know about salvation via these selected verses:

Romans 5:6 (NASB) says, "For while we were still helpless [sinners], at the right time Christ died for the ungodly." Helpless, Sinners, or Ungodly are the people of the world.

Newsflash: Children of God are people who may be living in this world, but they are ambassadors of Christ. Heaven is their true home (Philippians 3:20).

Romans 5:8 (NASB) says, "But God demonstrates His own love toward us, in that while we were yet sinners, Christ died for us."

Let us pause here for a moment. It is vital for you to know that before anyone begins to live in Christ and sees the Kingdom of God, that he or she must be born-again. Look at John 3:3-7 (NKJV): "Jesus answered and said to him, 'Most assuredly, I say to you, unless one is born-again, he cannot see the kingdom of God.' Nicodemus said to Him, 'How can a man be born when he is old? Can he enter a second time into his mother's womb and be born?' Jesus answered, 'Most assuredly, I say to you, unless one is born of water and the Spirit, he cannot enter the kingdom of God. That which is born of the flesh is flesh, and that which is born of the Spirit is spirit. Do not marvel that I said to you, You must be born-again.'"

Let's move on —

Jesus is a spiritual bridge between you and the Father God — for John 14:6 says, "No one can come to the Father except through me [Jesus]."

That selected verse briefly let us know that without Jesus, we are spiritually separated from God; He loves us and because of that, Jesus is the only way to connect us back to God. Once you find a Bible-based church, the pastor will be able to explain more than what I am sharing now. However, until then, keep this in your heart and mind, God loves every man and woman regardless of the color of his or her skin, not just the religious and the good. He does not love only the people who love Him. Check this, God loves everyone, even the unattractive and the unloving, the unbelieving and the stubborn, the self-centered and the greedy, the unpleasant and the unforgiving.

No matter what anyone of us has done or will ever do against God, He will always love us. God's love is His nature (1 John 4:8, 16) and that will never change. With that said, as mentioned John 3:16 earlier, God love was demonstrated towards us; He gave His only-begotten Son, Jesus to the world (people).

Let’s move on —

Romans 10:9 (NKJV) says, “…that if you confess with your mouth the Lord Jesus and believe in your heart that God has raised Him from the dead, you will be saved.” What an awesome opportunity this handbook presents for anyone to have without Christ that is to receive Him.

Let us do that right now. If you have never accepted Jesus as your Lord and Savior, you can do so, right now, by saying this: Heavenly Father, I thank you for Jesus. I confess and believe in my heart that Jesus is the Son of God, and God has raised Him from the dead. I confess Him now as my Lord and Savior. Jesus, thank you for coming into my life by saving me. And now, yes, I am saved!

Now praise God, and shout hallelujah! You are saved! You are now a child of God! Welcome to the body of Christ. By receiving Jesus Christ as your Lord and Savior, you have made an awesome decision. You have just joined other brothers and sisters who are also in the body of Christ (1 Corinthians 12:12). Again, welcome to being a part of, "… a chosen generation, a royal priesthood, a holy nation, His own special people, that you may proclaim the praises of Him who called you out of darkness into His marvelous light …," 1 Peter 2:9 (NKJV) You are a Child of God.

Child of God, this spiritual transaction that connects you with God is according to 2 Corinthians 5:17 (NKJV), where it says, "Therefore, if anyone [this is you] is in Christ, he is a new creation: old things have passed away; behold, all things have become new."

This has nothing to do with your flesh because what just happened was a spiritual transaction. You are not going to hear rocket blasts or see colorful balloons, or experience any other kinds of carnal celebrations that you may be used to in the natural. However, Heaven is rejoicing. According to Luke 15:7 (NASB), it says, "I tell you that in the same way, there will be more joy in Heaven over one sinner who repents than over ninety-nine righteous persons who need no repentance." Nevertheless, as you renew your mind, and this will be reaffirmed in subsequent chapters, your life in every area will begin to transform, more and more like Christ. This mind-renewing transformation is evident in doers of the Word. And that's what shows up on the outside of a child of God.

So get with a pastor, church leader, or a mature Christian to ask them about these verses.

Once again, congratulations and welcome to the body of Christ. You are a child of God. But get this, and it is vital, as of right now, and until you are with the Lord, no matter what you do in life, or what the world says about you, your name is forever written in the Lamb's Book of Life (Rev. 13:8 and 21:27). However, don't get it twisted, our actions from this point on should reflect a Christ-like life.

LET US PRAY…

Father, in the name of Jesus, I thank you for this person as he or she begins the journey of building a relationship with the Holy Spirit. I thank you that he or she will embark on a search for a pastor belonging to a Bible-based church as well as the renewing of his or her mind. I thank you that he or she has taken on the mind of Christ. I thank you that goodness and mercy will follow this child of God as he or she continues to increase in wisdom, status, and favor with God and with men (Luke 2:52). Additionally, I pray that favor surrounds him or her like a shield (Psalm 5:12). Father, I decree and declare that his or her purpose, identity, and destiny in Christ Jesus be fruitful in every area of life, and good works for the Kingdom of God. In Jesus' name, Amen!

CHAPTER TWO — A Brief Encouragement

Note On Being Born-Again

Wow, you are a new creature in Christ, meaning, you are one who is born-again. What an awesome position — to be in the body of Christ. Let me say this; when I accepted Christ, early on in my life, I didn't really understand what being born-again meant. From those around me, precious though they were, the only thing I knew about being born-again was that it meant I would be going to heaven. Other than that, I had no other particulars or biblical foundation.

I learned that being born-again meant much more than that. Sadly, on that front, I was not alone. Millions harbor misunderstandings on this — the decision to accept salvation. To do so is the most important decision a person will make in his or her life. Being born-again gets you to salvation. Salvation, if we really take it to heart, is the lifesaving gift from God that pushes us by faith through our trials and tribulations without complaining or disputing. As believers in Christ, rest in God. He's got your back, and He's got your future already planned out. He will stand in the gap for you, and shepherd (John 10:11) you to safety throughout your life journey. Trust Him.

One day while teaching prison inmates, I shared how early on in my Christian walk, I felt the need to do everything I could to win God's approval. I wanted to work in order to get brownie points from God. I wanted God to like me. I feared that if I ever slipped up in my walk, God was going to get me. Instant condemnation! As the old folks used to say when you did something wrong, "God's gonna strike you, dead!"

Instead of focusing on God's love and compassion, and His goodness and His mercies; I had misinterpreted Him as being a mean God, one who would punish me if I made a mistake. This notion often comes from the way we think, due to a lack of understanding. During the '60s and '70s this was my walk.

Today, I'm so glad to know that God is a loving God. And that He is not out to punish me, although God will chasten me because He loves me (Hebrews 12:6). This was good news for the incarcerated men to receive. It happened to be a diverse grouping of about seven grateful men, sitting in a classroom setting, reaching out to learn more about God. The teaching was well received. They asked more and more questions about how they could become born-again. I was grateful, too. In fact, I am grateful for my seven to eight years of serving incarcerated men and women behind bars.

During my early walk of being born-again, I was approached to do Prison Ministry by the church in which I attended at the time or someone I do not know today. This was around 1991 and 1992. I was also serving in the

U.S. Navy and stationed in Stockton, CA. But I was quickly dissuaded by another person who warned me that if I ventured inside of a prison, the evil spirits would jump on me. Sadly, I believed them, and walked away from that ministry. Fast forward to some sixteen years from that point, and light-years away from misunderstanding the Word of God, I believe I am walking in His plan and purpose for my life. Being born-again, and getting understanding, causes you to blossom into the abundant life that Jesus came to give (John 10:10).

I grew up in a single-parent household. My younger sister, Cynthia, and I were reared by my mother. And one of my earliest memories stems behind her rigid rule that if we did not go to church, we could not go outside to play. So Cynthia and I went to church. My point is, though, that it is not enough just to go to church, but it is paramount that you attend a Bible-based church. If you are rearing a young family take hold to what it says in Deuteronomy 6:5-9 (NKJV). It says, "You shall love the Lord your God with all your heart, with all your soul, and with all your strength. And these words which I command you today shall be in your heart. You shall teach them diligently to your children, and shall talk of them when you sit in your house, when you walk by the way, when you lie down, and when you rise up. You shall bind them as a sign on your hand, and they shall be as frontlets between your eyes. You shall write them on the doorposts of your house and on your gates."

With all that said, please know that I don't mean for my new revelations to be a punch in the face to all those teachers who may have erroneously taught many grandparents and parents decades ago, I simply want to make the point that once you know better, you do better — and that you should always seek to know better. Knowing and learning about the love of God, and everything about who you are in Him does matter. Being under the right leadership in a Bible-based church matters as well.

Child of God, remember how in Chapter One, we talked about how when you decide to give your life to Christ the pivotal changes may not be visible on the outside; e.g., if you are white, you will always be that in the natural, and those who are black will stay the same as well. But there is a monumental change on the inside. In this chapter, as we go over what it means to be born-again, please understand that your spiritual change continues through the transformation of renewing your mind. By faith that transformation will begin to change your natural attitudes, behaviors, and whatever else that is in need of change. Note: there is a section in this handbook about renewing your mind.

At the beginning of my Bible Study with the inmates, they were expecting to see an immediate change on the outside, but by the end of our sharing, they had a clearer understanding of the born-again transformation that would take place inside of them. I went on to say that being born-again is a spiritual change of having God's Spirit within us.

In addition, it was a spiritual rebirth; it was you and I, being BORN-AGAIN by the Spirit of God according to Titus 3:5. We are born from God, and given life, to live out the balance of our days in Christ Jesus.

Furthermore, I made it clear and plain to them by saying, "You too are a spirit (Genesis 2:7, 26, 27) living in a body." I believe it's vital for every believer to know this; especially those who are in the beginning journeys of their walk with God. Everyone needs to know that he or she is a spirit with a soul that lives in a body (1 Thessalonians 5:23).

Allow me to say it this way; as for a man or woman, you are a spiritual being that has a soul and resides in a house of flesh.

Check this out: The spirit of a man or a woman is for the purpose of having a relationship and communion with God, who is a Spirit. This is according to John 4:24 (NKJV). It says, "God is a Spirit and those who worship Him must worship in spirit and truth." Furthermore, about communion, 2 Corinthians 13:14 (NKJV) says, "The grace of the Lord Jesus Christ, and the love of God, and the communion of the Holy Spirit be with you all."

Now let us look into the structure of man and woman. This is good news because it brings a better understanding of knowing who you are in Christ's structure:

- Our *soul* is the *self* of man or woman. It contains our mind, will and emotions. Our *mind* involves our memory, imagination and reasoning. Our mind, as many have mentioned in several other books on this subject, is a battlefield. However, on that battlefield, Isaiah 26:3 (NKJV) says, "You will keep him in perfect peace, whose mind is stayed on You." Oh, by the way, that is one of the ways in which to win the battles that may take place in your mind — by keeping your mind on God via the Word of God.

- Our *will,* on the other hand, is the faculty of where he or she makes his or her decisions. I believe for us to make better decisions during our journey with God is to have some understanding before giving an answer or doing anything pertaining to living on Earth.
- Our *emotions,* for which we are responsible, are where we feel happiness, sadness, peace, joy, fear, anger, and/or depression, etc. This is worth repeating; our emotions are necessary and are

gifts from God. However, we must not allow our emotions to control us nor should we deny them. We put them in check based on the Word of God along with the help of the Holy Spirit.

- Our *bodies* function through the five senses, for which we are grateful unto God. They are a collective of the human system: touch, taste, smell, hearing, and seeing. Now it is important to keep these senses in check, especially, seeing and hearing. Because if not mindful, they can possibly cause a shipwreck of your faith, which could prevent you from moving forward with the Holy Spirit. To allow the world to flood your eyes and ears with unfruitful sights and words will possibly cause you to wander from the things of God. You will read more about that in Chapter Seven.
- Along with that, we cannot forget our *conscience,* which is where the Holy Spirit speaks (Romans

9:1) and *cognizance*. The *conscience* is our belief system, owning what we consider to be good and of moral integrity that lies between our spirit and soul. In addition, our *cognizance* is another vital part of us because it associates with our perception and awareness, which lies between our soul and the body.

Child of God, hopefully, what you've just read has provided understanding, and brought you some light. This brings me to give thanks to God — for Psalm 139:13-14 (NKJV) says, "For You [God] formed my inward parts; You [God] covered me in my mother's womb. I will praise You [*God*], for I am fearfully and wonderfully made; Marvelous are Your works, and that my soul knows very well." What an awesome God we serve. He has designed the body parts of man and woman to function the way that it does in this life on Earth.

Child of God, as we know, being born-again sets you and me free from bondage. It allows us as believers to witness to any and everyone who comes across our path. We are ambassadors of Christ for the Kingdom of God (2 Corinthians 5:20). It allows us to be who God created, called, and who He gifted us to be. Furthermore, understand that being born-again means that we are the light, salt, and reflection of the unseen God. He wants to be seen in and through us.

I am excited for what the Holy Spirit is doing. Moreover, I am excited because being born-again is an awesome way of life, and the beginning of a journey-walk with God. And that's not all! Through our constant fellowship with Jesus, we gain His divine guidance through life — through every trial, tribulation, life-valley moment, and moving-mountain experiences. He orchestrates our triumphs as well. Again, welcome to the body of Christ!

CHAPTER THREE — Not an Oops, a Mistake or an Accident!

Jesus took our shame that we share His glory!

Your birth was not an accident. God knows all things (1 John 3:20) and nothing gets by Him. Therefore, since God knows all things; then, knowing how you and I came to be was not a surprise to Him. Yeah, I know we've heard this before, we may have even expressed these sentiments, ourselves. How many times have you heard a parent say, "My youngest child was a surprise," or heard a mother say, "Yeah, my pills didn't work," or a father say, "My protection failed me." Well, to the world, this happens. But to God it's no surprise.

Perhaps you were conceived outside of the sanctity of marriage; if so, you are still not an accident. And if you have ever heard the term, *illegitimate child*, tagged onto your birth, rip it off. An accident is defined as an unforeseen and unplanned event or circumstance (Merriam-Webster.com). There are many people, out there, who think that their birth was an accident. However, based on God being all-knowing, this means that God knew the moment your mom and dad were going to have sex, causing you to enter this world.

Child of God, before we go any further, let's pause for a moment of prayer: Father, thank You that I am not an accident. Thank You that Jesus took my shame, and I've been set free from shame that I share His glory, in Jesus' name, Amen.

Now that you know that you are not an oops, a mistake or an accident — in life, you must also know that God has a plan, and that your life has a purpose. Jeremiah 29:11 (NLT) says, "For I know the plans I have for you, 'says the Lord.' They are plans for good and not for disaster, to give you a future and a hope." In 2 Timothy 1:9 (NKJV), it informs us of His purpose. It says, "Who has saved us and called *us* with a holy calling, not according to our works, but according to His own purpose and grace, which was given to us in Christ Jesus before time began."

God has a purpose, and you are to fulfill the purpose that He has personally placed on your life. Remember as a new creature, born-again, the Bible tells us, according to 2 Corinthians 5:17 (NKJV), "old things have passed away" (e.g., bad company, destructive habits, and works of the flesh, etc. [see Galatians 5:19-21]). You have changed, but the influence of the enemy will work to make you feel as if you haven't. The world has not changed, but you have. The proof that your change has begun shines in your attitude, the way you may dress, places you may go or refuse to go, people you hang around as well as those you refuse to be around. Because you are born-again, you no longer want to engage in things that you, now, consider ungodly. Living for Christ illuminates the concept of time; it's a gift. To waste it, is unprofitable for your life. You no longer want to live selfishly. Beware, and be prepared to hear people say, "I remember when you used to …" And when that happens, you can boldly say, "Thank God, I'm saved, delivered and set free because of knowing the Truth." (John 8:32)

Child of God, nevertheless, as you know, Satan, who is the enemy, a liar (John 8:44) and an accuser has been defeated because of Jesus. He continues to cause the people of the world to deny God, i.e., he blinds the mind of the unbeliever (2 Corinthians 4:4). This is exactly what is happening when we resist coming to God. This can also happen to those who have given their life to Christ, but who have strayed. I can remember holding on to the world/its value systems (1John 2:15-16) for dear life rather than to yield to the Spirit of God. I didn't want to give up any of my worldly vices such as drinking, nightclubbing, drugs, or anything that I engaged in during a time when I had walked away from the fellowship of God.

Yes, Satan can deceive the believer as well (2 Corinthians 11:3). Satan wants to cause the believer to deny the power of the Holy Spirit via his demonic influences. However, since he is defeated, as believers, we do not have to engage in a personal fight with Satan because Jesus has already taken care of that, and Satan knows that. There are some things that, as believers, we should do to ensure our victorious living. And please remember that through it all we also have the Holy Spirit and the Bible to help us. Check out these selected scriptures:

We resist evil — 1 Peter 5:8-9 (NKJV) says, "Be sober, be vigilant; because your adversary the devil walks about like a roaring lion, seeking whom he may devour. Resist him, steadfast in the faith …" and James 4:7 (NKJV) says, "Therefore submit to God. Resist the devil and he will flee from you."

Newsflash: Remember that you've just read that fighting Satan is not our battle. Please take another good read of the scripture you've just ingested. Understand that the scripture says to RESIST the devil, not FIGHT the devil. Why? Because Jesus has already taken care of that — at Calvary! Check out what apostle Paul said to the believers about resisting Satan. Ephesians 6:13-17 (NLT) says, "Therefore, put on every piece of God's armor so you will be able to resist the enemy in the time of evil. Then after the battle you will still be standing firm. Stand your ground, putting on the belt of truth and the body armor of God's righteousness. For shoes, put on the peace that comes from the Good News so that you will be fully prepared. In addition to all these, hold up the shield of faith to stop the fiery arrows of the devil. Put on salvation as your helmet, and take the sword of the Spirit, which is the Word of God." Child of God, this is our spiritual battle dress to go along with the Holy Spirit's help. With that said:

- We give no power to darkness, but we expose it — Ephesians 5:11 (NKJV) says, "And have no fellowship with the unfruitful works of darkness, but rather expose them." Check this, because you are valuable to the Kingdom of God, darkness is exposed when you come on the scene. Why? Because Matthew 5:14 (NKJV) says, "You are the light of the world. A city that is set on a hill cannot be hidden." In John 8:12 (NKJV) Jesus says, "I am the light of the world. He who follows Me shall not walk in darkness, but have the light of life." And Ephesians 5:8 (NKJV) says, "For you were once darkness, but now you are light in the Lord. Walk as children of light …" Because of Jesus and having the Holy Spirit in us, we are influenced by God, and we are capable to shine anywhere darkness abounds in this world.

- We act in faith and overcome evil with good — Romans 12:21 (NKJV) says, "Do not be overcome by evil, but overcome evil with good." Hey, treating all people with kindness will affect them greatly for the glory of God. It can also help you temper stress, high blood pressure, anxiety, and a host of other physical and emotional ailments. And oh, by the way, if you are dealing with any of these ailments, and the like, look at Isaiah 53:5 and 1 Peter 2:24.

We have this flesh. And we tend to get upset when, for example:

1. Someone in traffic cuts us off;
2. You're standing in the ten-items-or-less line because you're in a hurry, and the

person in front of you has thirty items. And then your cheeks are drawn tight when they turn to you and say, "You don't mind, do you?"

3. You ask the restaurant server, Christian-like, to prepare your steak medium rare, and he brings you shoe leather.

We should not react to negative situations or daily irritants with any finger signs or unfruitful words (1 Peter 2:23, 1 Peter 3:9). A person, acting in kindness, reflects spiritual growth and maturity to others — especially in the face of adversity. Amen? Need a little more strength? Give yourself a little chuckle, and let Matthew 5:16 pour into your spirit: "Let Your light so shine."

Along with that, we need to guard our words, and not speak the enemy's words of defeat. Child of God, just fight the good fight of faith (1 Timothy 6:12) that causes us to win in every area of life with God! But what I believe most importantly is what the apostle Paul said according to 2 Timothy 4:7 (NKJV). It says, “I have fought the good fight, I have finished the race, I have kept the faith.”

Hey, considering all that Jesus has done and gone through, and the challenges that the apostle Paul had to face to finish his course — let us finish what God has placed in us to do. Amen? That is why this handbook, *In All Your Getting, Get Understanding!* is designed to give the newly born-again Christian a far better start on his or her journey with God. Furthermore, *Get Understanding* can enhance the journeys of mature Christians as well.

Let us not stop here. You also have been given a gift from God, according to 1 Peter, 4:10 (NKJV). It says, “As each one has received a gift, minister it to one another, as good stewards of the manifold grace of God.” Lastly, every born-again Christian has been given everything he or she needs to win and finish his or her assignment on Earth. According to 2 Peter, 1:3 (NJKV), it says, "… as His divine power has given to us all things that pertain to life and godliness through the knowledge of Him who called us by glory and virtue ...."

The body of Christ has what it takes to live out and fulfill God's given purpose on Earth. So as you read *In All Your Getting, Get Understanding!* you now know that you are not an accident. God has a plan and your life has a purpose. Please know that while you are here on Earth, you have the power to live the abundant life that Jesus came to give (John 10:10), which encompasses your godly assignments within that purpose.

God is the creator of all things according to Colossians 1:16 (NKJV), where it says, "For by Him all things were created that are in heaven and that are on Earth, visible and invisible, whether thrones or dominions or principalities or powers. All things were created through

Him and for Him." We all came from God, as He is the creator. You and I need to go to God about everything concerning us. Just like *Campbell Soup* knows every ingredient it adds to its products, God knows everything He has placed inside of us. That is why it is vital to go to God about your purpose as well as your godly assignments in life as a whole, on Earth.

One of the many important things that you must learn during this journey is how to constantly commune (i.e., talk and fellowship) with God to discover just what God's purpose is for your life. We can have abundant living, a successful family life and a successful career life, but without living in God's purpose, our existence on Earth is really lifeless. None of your earthly accomplishments even matter. Hey, we must seek God to know, learn and do what He purposes us to do. To do so means to enjoy the blessings that come with our obedience to God.

Lastly, as the Word says, according to Jeremiah 1:5 (NLT), "I knew you before I formed you in your mother's womb." As God knew Jeremiah, He knew you too! God knows everything and nothing gets by Him, especially your birth into this world, which was not an accident!

Now move on with no regrets because Jesus died for everything that you and I will ever face in this life. As you move on *In All Your Getting, Get Understanding!* I have a chapter about the Holy Spirit, who has been assigned to help you on your journey. So get ready by keeping your mind on God, while reading *Get Understanding*. I believe that you will experience encounters with God via the Holy Spirit's presence as well as enjoy life-changing victories. Your life will never be the same again, in Jesus' name, Amen!

CHAPTER FOUR — The Measure of Faith

Every born-again believer in Christ has faith!

Child of God, something I discovered, based on my early walk with God, happened to be a very important factor. And that is understanding how the measure of faith fits in one's life. Most people of God, and perhaps the church that a new believer may attend, may unintentionally neglect to explain how to live by faith. Let me tell you right now — you have enough faith to be, do and have everything God said. How is this, you might ask? It's because it has already been instilled in you, by you accepting Jesus Christ.

I believe this chapter is so vital for everyone walking with God. Not that all the other chapters are not important; however, faith is the key to pleasing God (Hebrews 11:6). It is needed like the air we breathe to stay alive. And if anything else tries to replace it, like someone using an oxygen tank to breathe, sooner or later, that tank will go empty. An empty tank is the same as having an empty life without faith. Without it you will choke and die. No air, no breath. No faith, no life. The *just* (Christians) shall live by faith. Also know that faith is the gift (Ephesians 2:8) that God imparted to every born-again person.

Since God gave us faith as a gift, then, what is faith? According to Hebrews 11:1 (NLT), the Bible says, "It is the confident assurance that what we hope for is going to happen. It is the evidence of things we cannot yet see." Also, according to 2 Corinthians 4:18 (NCV) it says, "We set our eyes not on what we see but on what we cannot see. What we see will last only a short time, but what we cannot see will last forever."

Child of God, just by reading those two selected verses I can say, faith is visualizing what you see in your spirit based on what the Word of God has already said about you, and about whatever you may be going through.

For example, faith is the evidence of things unseen, in an unseen world that is moving and working in your life via the help of the Holy Spirit. One of the ways to know that the Holy Spirit is with you, besides knowing that God has given Him to you, is also knowing that you can trust Him in revealing God's truth. Such acknowledgment of the unseen supplies the fuel that keeps you moving in a positive direction or standing firm in the midst of a trial. Now that's faith! Beloved, I had to see myself graduating from college, based on Philippians 4:13, boldly stating, "I can do all things through Christ who strengthens me."

Faced with the challenges of rearing a family and struggling to overcome the fear of failure as well as the negative predictions that others had pronounced on my life, it was my growing measure of faith, working inside of me that pushed me through. When I failed a subject, and had to take two different math classes to prepare for college-level math, I had to encourage myself in the Lord. I invoked my faith, unseen; and declared, out loud, what the Word of God said.

My back-to-school journey was a tough one. And the closer I got to the finish line, the tougher it became. Still, in bold faith, about eight or nine months away from graduation, I began to rehearse what I wanted to say to those who had helped me along the way. Why? It was because by faith, the evidence of what we want to accomplish in life is in our heart. And we should use that unseen evidence to keep us moving in that direction no matter what it takes — we have faith!

Hey, visualization in your spirit is vital! So please let us not magnify the challenges that we may be facing in our lives. Instead, let us lift up the name of Jesus and thank Him for being the source of life, and the answer to our challenges. All things are possible with God (Matthew 19:26) and we win (1 Corinthians 15:57)!

Romans 12:3, tells us that, "God has dealt to each one a measure of faith." So it doesn't matter where we come from or the color of our skin, or the money we have, or even the lack thereof; God gave each believer a measure of faith. This measure of faith is sufficient for the believer.

Now this is where you and I need to gain understanding and to get it fast because everything we do on Earth, as Kingdom kids, works by faith. The Word of God tells us that the *just* (Christians) shall live by faith (Habakkuk 2:4, Romans 1:17, Galatians 3:11, Hebrews 10:38).

With that said, we need to know the difference between having faith and using it. Having faith is what God has already given every believer in Christ according to Romans 12:3. However, using it is really up to you, and not God, because of the free will we have to make our own choices and to live by our own consequences. As free-will people, please know that God does not force us to do anything. We have the choice whether or not to accept the Holy Spirit's direction. When you and I know the Word of God, which is His will for our lives, but we do not follow it, we are resisting the Holy Spirit's assignment in our lives.

Check this out: We are responsible for our own actions. Our daily choices lead to daily consequences, good or bad. So with that said, no matter how we look at it, we are still responsible for our actions; and even, in many cases, we are responsible for our inactions as well. For example, those who smoke cigarettes are familiar with cigarette package labels giving fair warning about how the act of smoking can possibly harm a smoker's health. Therefore, armed with that information, there is an individual responsibility to be had based on one's choice to smoke or not to smoke.

Another example, after your physical examination, the doctor tells you to lose some weight because you are at risk for chronic disease, such as high blood, diabetes or other related challenges. Well, you've disregarded the instructions, and before long here comes the added medication, and all the problems that come along with chronic ailments.

And finally, let's say for example that your rent, mortgage note, gas bill, electric bill or whatever else bill is due every first of the month. Let's also say that you don't have enough money to reach all of your first-of-the-month responsibilities. Why? Because you chose to spend money on your wants, and not your needs.

All that has happened because you and I, as individuals, have at one time or another, disregarded our responsibilities, our good-common sense, and godly wisdom. And if that wasn't enough, when the consequence comes, we want to blame Satan for our behavior. We allow excuses to continue to lead us into defeated areas of life.

Prayerfully, our choices will be based on the Word of God. Faith is not to be used like a spare tire, or like a spoon only to be grabbed when needed. Faith is constantly active in what we believe the Word of God says 24/7, every year throughout the balance of our days on Earth. So, you have it and you must use it no matter what is going on in your life. Know this, let's not get it twisted! Faith neither removes nor replaces your responsibility. However, faith helps you to step up to your responsibility in life, and your outcome will glorify God.

Child of God, as you had read every believer has been given a measure of faith. However, it is up to every believer to exercise his or her faith. Remember faith is the believer's way of life, and he or she must feed their faith constantly by hearing the Word of God (Romans 10:17). Additionally, acting on what he or she heard, learned and understands by being a doer of the Word (James 1:22). Check this, faith is like a muscle. It can grow weak or it can be strengthened, depending on how much you and I use it.

Oh, by the way, since the *just* (Christians) shall live by faith then, read and meditate on these verses:

- Deuteronomy 31:6 (NKJV) — "Be strong and of good courage, do not fear nor be afraid of them; for the Lord your God, He is the One who goes with you. He will not leave you nor forsake you."
- Proverbs 3:5 (NJKV) — "Trust in the Lord with all your heart, and lean not on your own understanding; in all your ways acknowledge Him, and He shall direct your paths."

- Isaiah 26:3 (NKJV) — "You will keep him in perfect peace, whose mind is stayed on You, because he trusts in You."
- Isaiah 41:10 (NKJV) — "… Fear not, for I am with you; be not dismayed, for I am your God. I will strengthen you, yes, I will help you, I will uphold you with My righteous right hand.'"
- Mark 11:20-24 (NKJV) — "Now in the morning, as they passed by, they saw the fig tree dried up from the roots. And Peter, remembering, said to Him, 'Rabbi, look! The fig tree which You cursed has withered away.' So Jesus answered and said to them, 'Have faith in God. For assuredly, I say to you, whoever says to this mountain, Be removed and be cast into the sea, and does not doubt in his heart, but believes that those things he says will be done, he will have whatever he

says. Therefore I say to you, whatever things you ask when you pray, believe that you receive them, and you will have them.'"

- Hebrews 10:23 (NKJV) — "Let us hold fast the confession of our hope without wavering, for He who promised is faithful."
- Hebrews 11:1 (NKJV) — "Now faith is the substance of things hoped for, the evidence of things not seen."
- Hebrews 11:6 (NKJV) — "But without faith it is impossible to please Him, for he who comes to God must believe that He is, and that He is a rewarder of those who diligently seek Him."
- Hebrews 12:2 (NKJV) — "… looking unto Jesus, the author and finisher of our faith, who for the joy that was set before Him endured the cross,

despising the shame, and has sat down at the right hand of the throne of God."

- James 1:6 (NKJV) — "But let him ask in faith, with no doubting, for he who doubts is like a wave of the sea driven and tossed by the wind."
- 1 John 5:4 (NKJV) — "For whatever is born of God overcomes the world. And this is the victory that has overcome the world — our faith."

Well, you have it and I want to enforce it one more time but in another way of saying it. Faith is an imperative key to accessing and receiving the recourses we need, and from the main source, our God!

CHAPTER FIVE — HELLO HOLY SPIRIT

The Holy Spirit gives the believer the ability to live for Christ in every area of his or her life.

Now, before we go into looking for a pastor with a Bible-based church, and renewing our mind, I want to mention someone rarely mentioned during a person's early walk with God. While it could be safe to say that most people have heard about God, and that most have heard about Jesus, often, not many have heard about the Holy Spirit. The Holy Spirit is our guide on Earth. Jesus, before He was crucified, said something that was so vital, pertaining to our walk on Earth. He said, according to John 14:16 (NLT), "And I will ask the Father, and He will give you another Advocate who will never leave you [other Bible translations refer to the 'Advocate' as Helper, Comforter, Counselor]." Check this, in John 16:7 (NKJV), Jesus also said, "Nevertheless I tell you the truth. It is to your advantage that I go away; for if I do not go away, the Helper will not come to you; but if I depart, I will send Him to you." Did you catch that? Jesus is saying that it is for the believer's advantage that the Holy Spirit should come and live in us.

Child of God, the moment you accepted Jesus as your Lord and Savior, the Holy Spirit came into you, and according to 1 Corinthians 6:17, we became one spirit with Him. Everything you need for this life on Earth, God has already given to you, according to 2 Peter 1:3 (NKJV). This scripture says, "… as His divine power has given to us all things that pertain to life and godliness." Additionally, it says in Ephesians 1:3 (NKJV), "Blessed be the God and Father of our Lord Jesus Christ, who has blessed us with every spiritual blessing in the heavenly places in Christ." Everything you and I will ever need on Earth; God has already given us, which includes the Holy Spirit. Therefore, the Holy Spirit resides in every born-again believer so that the power of our awesome God can flow in, and through us.

For example, when I retired from the U.S. Navy, I experienced about a three-month challenge to find somewhere to live, and a suitable job that would support my family. It was challenging, but I held on to my faith. Seemingly out of the blue, but not really, of course, a friend, a fellow sailor who had been stationed with me in Japan, contacted me. He contacted me to do a favor for a friend of his. My friend shared that a neighbor of his was moving on to another job, but had to first find a replacement for the position he was currently in. Mmm! Look at the favor of God (Psalm 5:12).

I did not have experience in that position, but I got the job. Thank you God. I took on the responsibility of learning and growing into that job, which, at times, proved rough, but God kept me. And my faith kept me going. On top of that, I met another friend, a shipmate whom I hadn't seen in more than twenty years, prior. He just popped up and offered me and my wife a place to stay — until we could find permanent housing. Wow, God is faithful and true to His Word. Philippians 4:19 (NKJV) says, "And my God shall supply all your need according to His riches and glory by Christ Jesus." The Holy Spirit through the Word of God taught me a great life lesson. It taught me to stop trying to do things on my own and to learn how to depend on Him.

By trusting the Holy Spirit in me, I learned that I cannot do anything without God (John 15:5). And if I submit to the leading of the Holy Spirit, He flows through me, and on that power, "I can do all things through Christ, who strengthens me (Philippians 4:13)." Now that's the power of our awesome God flowing in us. Let us not stop here. Please don't be shy when it comes to asking the Holy Spirit for guidance. Be assured that the Holy Spirit will help to see your dreams become reality, your goals accomplished, and He will help you to achieve those godly desires of your heart. It says in Psalm 37: 4 (NKJV), "Delight yourself also in the Lord, and He shall give you the desires of your heart." Child of God, by you delighting yourself in the ways of God, the Holy Spirit will place ideas in your heart that will move you forward, give you blueprints for your plans, and place innovations down in your soul — privy to only you. Increase your prayer life, consistently read and study the Bible, and spend ample time communing with the Holy Spirit to learn His voice.

The Holy Spirit is your witness and guarantee of being a Child of God. Check this out: According to 2 Corinthians 1:22 (NKJV) the latter part of it says, "… given us the Spirit in our hearts as a guarantee."

Wow, what an awesome God who loves us so much He gave us His guarantee in our hearts. Here are more scriptures about the Holy Spirit, residing within us that God has given to the body of Christ:

- Romans 8:16 (NLT), "For His Spirit joins with our spirit to affirm that we are God's children."
- Galatians 4:6 (NIV), "Because you are his sons, God sent the Spirit of His Son into our hearts, the Spirit who calls out, Abba, Father."
- 1 John 3:24 (NLT), "Those who obey God's commandments remain in fellowship with him, and he with them. In addition, we know he lives in us because the Spirit he gave us lives in us."
- 1 John 4:13 (NLT), "And God has given us his Spirit as proof that we live in him and he in us."

Child of God, God loves us so much He wanted to live within us via the Holy Spirit. Furthermore, the latter part of 2 Corinthians 3:18 (NLT) says, "the Lord who is the

Spirit makes us more and more like Him as we are changed into his glorious image."

This is some vital and exciting information! The magnificent work, the Holy Spirit is doing in the believer's life is great for the believer to know. So, while the Holy Spirit is at work, be sure to know, it is your responsibility as God's son or daughter to get to know the Holy Spirit who is assigned to your life. He is doing great things in our lives, while we are being transformed into Christ-like character, day-by-day, not wasting a second.

Hey, get this in your thinking, as a born-again believer, you and I have an awesome responsibility to take this gift, seriously. As the Holy Spirit works in our lives, understand that the world is watching us. In fact, everywhere we go people are watching us, especially the unbelievers. So since they need to see God, we are the men and women that God uses to reveal himself to the masses. How you and I carry ourselves, i.e., in our neighborhoods, on the job, or in public places in general, keep in mind that we are ambassadors (2 Corinthians 5:20), representatives of the Kingdom of God.

Let's move on —

There's something else I believe you should know. Most seasoned people of God already know this fact. However, the newest born-again Christian, just starting out, may not yet have a strong sense of understanding that the Holy Spirit is real. In addition, a new born-again believer may not understand that the Holy Spirit is actually living within him or her. Though you may not be able to see the Holy Spirit; in fact, it is tangible inside of you. According to Romans 8:11(NKJV) the same Spirit that raised Jesus is living in every believer who received Christ as Lord and Savior.

Here's what that verse 11 says, "but if the Spirit of Him who raised Jesus from the dead dwells in you, He who raised Christ from the dead will also give life to our mortal bodies through His Spirit who dwells in you." The same power in Christ is in you as God's son or daughter! Although, God's Spirit gives life to our mortal body, our earthly temple, we will have an immortal body when Jesus returns. Therefore, in the meantime, we receive the Life of God in our earthly body by faith. Let us continue by seeing more selected verses about God via the Holy Spirit that is in every believer:

- John 14:23 (NKJV), "Jesus answered and said to him, 'If anyone loves Me, he will keep My word; and My Father will love him, and We will come to him and make Our home with him.'"
- Romans 8:9 (NKJV), "But you are not in the flesh but in the Spirit, if indeed the Spirit of God dwells in you. Now if anyone does not have the Spirit of Christ, he is not His."

- 1 Corinthians 3:16 (GNT), "Surely you know that you are God's temple and that God's Spirit lives in you!"
- 1 Corinthians 6:19-20 (GNT), "Don't you know that your body is the temple of the Holy Spirit, who lives in you and who was given to you by God? You do not belong to yourselves but to God; he bought you for a price. So use your bodies for God's glory."

Let us stop here for a moment. The verse you just read says that you were bought with a price. It cost God's only-begotten Son, Jesus. His life for ours, today, yesterday, and forever more, came at a price for which no man can repay. Do you know how valuable you are to God? God so loves us that He knows the number of hairs on your head (Matthew 10:30). Wow, even the follicles on a person's baldhead is known to God. However, God at the same time knows everything about you, and what

He has placed in you. You are worth more than any amount of money on Earth. Your body is not cheap, it is priceless! So don't settle for less and be godly proud with a smile to be born-again.

As a child of God, remember, you are not what someone may declare you are, and you are not an Oops! You are not a mistake that happened to life. Sadly, a person may have heard his or her family member cast them down by saying, "You are no good for nothing." Or they may have heard throughout their lives, "You will never 'mount-up to anything." Or, even worse, yet, a person may have been condemned by hearing a family member say, "You're just like your father …" or, "You're just like your mother … You're sorry and worthless in life." Child of God, don't listen to any of that. As a matter of fact, cast those negative opinions down. Release them from your mind and heart. In the words of my pastor, Dr. Michael Freeman, "Divorce yourself from the opinions of others." Dr. Freeman is the senior pastor of *Spirit of Faith Christian Center* in Temple Hills, Maryland. You are fearfully and wonderfully made. You are a man or woman of God with power and authority in Jesus' name! You are who God says you are, and nothing less than that! In 2 Corinthians 10:4-5, it says, "For the weapons of our warfare are not carnal but mighty in God for pulling down strongholds, casting down arguments and every high thing that exalts itself against the knowledge of God, bringing every thought into captivity to the obedience of Christ …" With that said, child of God, do not allow negative, foolish talk or anything that goes against God's Word to nest in your mind. **Cast it down!**

Let's move on —

Child of God, each believer in the body of Christ cannot successfully operate apart from the Holy Spirit. Now a person may try or temporarily feel as if he or she is progressing in this world under his or her understanding (Proverbs 3:5). It is the power of the Holy Spirit at work in the believer, and not the strength of anyone to do the work of the Lord, alone (John 15:5). We as believers must depend upon the Holy Spirit while obeying the Word of God for what we do on Earth for the sake of the Kingdom of God.

With that said, you should know the Holy Spirit is indeed a divine person because He possesses a mind, emotion, and a will. Read these selective verses:

- Romans 8:26-27 tells us the Holy Spirit intercedes for us.
- 1 Corinthians 2:10 tells us the Holy Spirit thinks and knows.
- 1 Corinthians 12:7-11 tells us the Holy Spirit makes decisions according to His will.

- Ephesians 4:30 tells us the Holy Spirit can be grieved.

In the coming pages, you will read more about how we can grieve the Holy Spirit, later, as I briefly explain being filled with the Holy Spirit. Knowing about the Holy Spirit's assignment in every believer's life, John 16:13 (NLT) says, "When the Spirit of truth comes, He will guide you into all truth. He will not speak on His own but will tell you what He has heard. He will tell you about the future." Wow, the Spirit of truth never leads you and me into untruth. I believe the Holy Spirit will tell us the things that will lead us toward destiny, that will lead us to the abundant life Jesus talked about in John 10:10, and to the things that will benefit others for the Kingdom's sake. Consequently, as anything else regarding your walk with God, the Holy Spirit is a key person to know and to spend time with. Here are other selective scriptures you can read:

- John 7:39 (NASB) — "But this He spoke of the Spirit, whom those who believed in Him were to receive; for the Spirit was not yet [given], because Jesus was not yet glorified."
- John 14:26 (NLT) — "But when the Father sends the Advocate as My representative — that is, the Holy Spirit — He will teach you everything and will remind you of everything I have told you."
- John 15:26 (NASB) — "When the Helper comes, whom I will send to you from the Father, that is the Spirit of truth who proceeds from the Father, He will testify about Me."

Child of God, as mentioned earlier, every Christian has the Helper living on the inside of him or her. However, every Christian is neither listening to Him nor following His way of doing things via the Word of God. This is an important note: Although we are different individuals, we are carrying the same Holy Spirit inside of us because we have accepted Jesus as Lord and Savior in our lives!

For that reason, as you walk with God, led by the Holy Spirit via the Word of God, your understanding of the Holy Spirit increases. As your understanding increases, you will gain more of an appreciation and a gratefulness for the Kingdom lifestyle. Oh, by the way, regarding the Kingdom, according to Luke 17:21b (NKJV), it says, "For indeed, the kingdom of God is within you."

Child of God, in all your getting to get understanding know that what has already been placed in you will cause your life to reflect love, joy, peace, longsuffering (patience), kindness, goodness, faithfulness, gentleness, and self-control (Galatians 5:22-23). Those around you will see how God's way of doing things works well in every area of your life — here on Earth! Such evidence can win others for Christ (Proverbs 11:30).

The Bible says according to 2 Peter 1:3 (NKJV), "His divine power has given to us (believers) all things that pertain to life and godliness through the knowledge of Him who called us by glory and virtue." So let me say it another way, get a keen understanding of what God has already placed in you!

Hey, since the Holy Spirit is our guide on Earth, every child of God should consider Him as the Divine, easy-to-navigate *Worldwide Positioning System.* It's his or her personal *WPS,* built-strong for life on Earth. Your *WPS,* engineered by God, will always be with you, never to steer you in the wrong direction (John 16:13). In addition, He stays in sync throughout all parts of the world without weekly, monthly or yearly updates. The only thing for you to do, as a believer, is to spend quality time reading your Bible, meditating on the Word of God, and increasing your prayer life.

Also, and this is key, during my beginning walk with God, one of the first things I heard was to never question God. Now, bless the dear hearts of the older saints who taught me this, but after years of being afraid to question God, I finally learned that I could go to Him with my questions because I'm His child. For example, I grew up with friends who had a father in their household, while I had no father living with me. I watched my best buddies go on trips with their dads, and there I was unable to do the same thing. And for many years, hurt and feeling alone, I wondered why. I had questions why I didn't have a father living with me — a father, in our home, who loved me. I had questions. But I was taught, never to question God.

It is possible that the psychological effects of our teenage experiences can have a great impact on who we are, and who we become later in life. Sadly, I knew that I had questions to ask God, but I held back because I was afraid of God. I feared I would be punished. Being repeatedly told that questioning God was something that we should not do, or better not do, only caused added pain and confusion inside of me.

Child of God, if you grew up without having a father or mother around to guide and nourish you, please know this — that with God all things are possible (Matthew 19:26). Yes, you do have the power of the Holy Spirit; however, you also have to believe you can overcome the unfavorable circumstances that comes along with growing up without a father or mother. Believe that you can still move on toward your god-filled destiny. Additionally, if this was the case for you, and now you are a father or mother, you know what to do. Be there and cherish every precious moment with your family.

I finally understood that He was, and is, big enough to handle whatever I have to ask, in whatever way in which I ask it just like Martha did in John 11:21. Child of God, each generation should go further than the last, ask those questions to seek initial understanding on God's Word or on how you should live your life, or get clarity for what you believe that you already understand. Amen.

Your personal *WPS,* which is the Holy Spirit, will also inform you of the things you need to know as you ask questions. He will prepare you for what's ahead, and remind you about what you've already learned during your journey; you do not have to worry about spending money because there are no batteries required. Lastly, your *WPS* will never lose a signal and will always run at full power. Because your *WPS* is sourced from the manufacture, Himself, God.

Now since we are getting understanding and were just thinking about the Holy Spirit being our Divine *WPS*, it's important for you to know that the Holy Spirit is not an *it*. Let's be clear, the Holy Spirit is a *He*. Look how John 14:15-17 (NKJV) identifies the Holy Spirit, he says, "If you love Me, keep My commandments. And I will pray the Father, and He will give you another Helper, that He may abide with you forever the Spirit of truth, whom the world cannot receive, because it neither sees Him nor knows Him; but you know Him, for He dwells with you and will be in you."

So, as you and I continue our on-going conversations with the Holy Spirit, it is important to stay in the Word of God. Why? Because that is one of the ways, the Holy Spirit speaks to us.

And by the way, let's not get spooky or act like weird and/or super-spiritual people regarding our walk with God. The Holy Spirit does not speak with audible words. However, He leads us through our own conscience (Romans 9:1). Therefore, we need to know the Word of God so that whenever He speaks, the Word speaks as well, in agreement with what He is saying and doing in our lives.

Through the Holy Spirit, using the Word of God, we are not only encouraged, but also the Holy Spirit helps us to accomplish our goals, connect us with godly ideals, even renders to us the godly desires of our hearts, in the ways that cannot be accomplished in the natural. The Holy Spirit, our *WPS*, can guide us toward our dreams. He hears and protects our hearts when we are in tune with Him. Additionally, the Holy Spirit will speak God's plans for our lives — stretching, locally and globally.

Child of God, keep this constantly in your mind and heart, the Holy Spirit has been ordered to follow God's assignment in each believer. He always obeys, in spite of whatever is going on throughout the Earth. He will never leave nor forsake a believer no matter what is going on. In other words, He will abide with you forever (John 14:16).

Let us pray here, "Father, thank you for the Holy Spirit who is my helper on Earth. Holy Spirit, I want to know You in every area of my life. Thank you for being in me every step of my life journey on Earth — that together I can do the things of God that will glorify Him in Jesus' name, Amen!"

Lastly, the Holy Spirit will help you find a pastor with a Bible-based church and teach you through the renewing of your mind to think like the kings and priests, which we are in Christ (1 Peter 2:9, Revelation 1:5-6 & 5:10).

Nevertheless, before we go any further, looking for a pastor with a Bible-based church, let me add this about the Holy Spirit, it is a command for every believer to be filled with the Holy Spirit. Look at these selective verses, which talks about being filled with the Holy Spirit:

- Luke 1:15 (NKJV), "For he will be great in the sight of the Lord, and shall drink neither wine nor strong drink. He will also be filled with the Holy Spirit, even from his mother's womb."

- Luke 1:41 (NKJV), "And it happened, when Elizabeth heard the greeting of Mary, that the babe leaped in her womb; and Elizabeth was filled with the Holy Spirit."
- Luke 1:67 (NKJV), "Now his father Zacharias was filled with the Holy Spirit, and prophesied."
- Luke 4:1 (NKJV), "Then Jesus, being filled with the Holy Spirit, returned from the Jordan and was led by the Spirit into the wilderness."
- Acts 2:4 (NKJV), "And they were all filled with the Holy Spirit and began to speak with other tongues, as the Spirit gave them utterance."
- Acts 4:8 (NKJV), "Then Peter, filled with the Holy Spirit, said to them, "Rulers of the people and elders of Israel."
- Acts 4:31 (NKJV), "And when they had prayed, the place where they were assembled together was

shaken; and they were all filled with the Holy Spirit, and they spoke the Word of God with boldness."

- Acts 6:5 (NKJV), "And the saying pleased the whole multitude. And they chose Stephen, a man full of faith and the Holy Spirit …"
- Acts 7:55 (NKJV), "But he, being full of the Holy Spirit, gazed into heaven and saw the glory of God, and Jesus standing at the right hand of God."
- Acts 9:17 (NKJV), "And Ananias went his way and entered the house; and laying hands on him he said, 'Brother Saul, the Lord Jesus, who appeared to you on the road as you came, has sent me that you may receive your sight and be filled with the Holy Spirit'"

- Acts 13:9 (NKJV), “Then Saul, who also is called Paul, filled with the Holy Spirit, looked intently at him.”
- Acts 13:52 (NKJV), “And the disciples were filled with joy and with the Holy Spirit.”

Now, keep in mind, when you accepted Jesus Christ as your Lord and Savior, the Holy Spirit was given to you at the same time. This is vital information to know, along with everything else pertaining to your life on Earth. Let us look at the command according to Ephesians 5:18 in three different translations about being filled with the Holy Spirit:

- Amplified translation verse says, “Do not get drunk with wine, for that is wickedness (corruption, stupidity), but be filled with the [Holy] Spirit *and* constantly guided by Him.”

- Good News Translation verse says, "Do not get drunk with wine, which will only ruin you; instead, be filled with the Spirit."
- New King James Version translation verse says, "and do not be drunk with wine, in which is dissipation; but be filled with the Spirit."

So, what does it mean to be filled with the Holy Spirit? And why did the apostle Paul say the following, "Do not be drunk with wine,"? These two questions are great to ask because it shows direction toward getting understanding.

Let us look at the word *drunk*. According to the dictionary *drunk* means, "being in a temporary state in which one's physical and mental faculties are impaired by an excess of alcoholic drink; intoxicated." **http://www.dictionary.com/browse/drunk**. Referencing the scripture, one could surmise that this translates to a lack of control. However, when the scripture refers to *being filled*, this translates to the utmost, highest degree of the Holy Spirit's control of our spiritual walk. We give Him full permission to guide and influence our lives, according to what the Word of God says.

Oh, by the way, 1 Peter 5:8 (NKJV) says, "Be sober, be vigilant; because your adversary the devil walks about like a roaring lion, seeking whom he may devour." Check this out: one of the definitions for the word *sober* means not to become intoxicated with alcohol or drugs.

So in short, we can understand that a drunken influence can lead to the wrong path in life, making unwise decisions. Being filled with the Holy Spirit's influence and obeying the Word of God can help the children of God make wise decisions. Which brings me to say, being filled or knowing that you are already with the Holy Spirit helps a child of God to walk in the Spirit, and not fulfill the lust of the flesh (Galatians 5:16). When you and I walk in the Spirit by the Word, we cannot please the flesh. Only when we walk outside of the Word, our flesh is pleased in this world. According to scripture, we are told, "Do not be conformed to this world …" (Romans 12:2).

Lastly, when we are filled with the Spirit, we are controlled by Him and we have steadiness to maintain the course of life with God. We do not give up in life neither should we quit and throw in the towel. We should not say that as born-again believers, we are defeated. Because, in 1 John 4:4 (NKJV), it says, "… He who is in you is greater than he who is in the world."

Child of God, as it has been mentioned several times throughout these pages thus far that understanding is what we are after. According to Habakkuk 2:4, Romans 1:17, Galatians 3:11 and Hebrews 10:38 as believers our walk with God is by faith. So, believe God that you are filled with the Holy Spirit. However, because we walk by faith and not by sight, you must understand that being filled with the Holy Spirit is neither a mere emotional experience nor is it a theatrical or Hollywood extravaganza with stars searing through the sky or a loud blast. What it is, is just an earnest act of your faith, believing what our Heavenly Father has already put inside of you. And it is life-changing. Remember, Ephesians 1:3, and according to 2 Peter 1:3 (NLT), "By his divine power, God has given us everything we need for living a godly life."

Child of God, this is a faith-walk with God. Being filled with the Holy Spirit is an awesome way of life and should be ongoing. Therefore, talk with God about being filled with the Holy Spirit. Believe that you are filled with the Holy Spirit and allow Him to control your life by obeying the Word of God that leaves no room for you to do things on your own. Oh, let me say this, in life, God already knows about the problem, the mistakes, the downfalls, the pitfalls or whatever involves sin in everyone's life. He knows everything that has happened and everything that will happen. Nevertheless, when or if we sin, without delay confess and repent (1 John 1:9) it to God. Furthermore, believe you are forgiven and move on by obeying the Word, being filled and Spirit-led (Romans 8:14).

Let us pray: Father, we are thankful for Jesus! Because of Him, sin has been crucified upon the cross, and now by faith in Jesus "we have redemption through His blood, the forgiveness of sins, according to the riches of His grace" (Ephesians 1:7). Thank you, Father, for knowing each of our lives from the beginning to the end that no matter what we do, your love for each of us will never change (Romans 8:38-39) in Jesus' name, AMEN!

Earlier, I mentioned about not grieving the Holy Spirit. The Bible also says, do not "quench" the Holy Spirit (Ephesians 4:30 & 1 Thessalonians 5:19). When either of those instances take place, it means that a person is preventing the Holy Spirit to take full control. When that happens, the Holy Spirit cannot fully reveal himself to us. When you and I grieve or quench the Holy Spirit, we are not allowing Him to be in full control of our life. Keep this in mind; the Spirit of God will never violate our will.

Now as the command is given in Ephesians 5:18, you are filled with the Spirit and this is a step-by-step, day-to-day, moment-to-moment walk with God. As you believe, and based on the act of your faith, thank the Father for what He has already placed in you by faith. Now allow Him to take control, while you obey the Word of God. Amen!

Child of God, "That's why the change has taken place in your life when you accepted Jesus. That's why there's something new in your life. The Spirit of God is there. And He is there not only to empower you, and not only to fill you for service, not only to equip you for ministry, not only to function through the gifts that God has given you, but He's there to guarantee your inheritance" (https://www.gty.org/library/sermons-library/1905/divine-promises-guaranteed).

Oh, by the way since you are reaching out and getting to know the Holy Spirit in your life, let's not lie to Him. Check this out: Here are four verses that reflect a clear understanding about lying to the Holy Spirit being the same as lying to God. Look at Acts 5:1-4 and see how the disciple Peter confronts Ananias, "But a certain man named Ananias, with Sapphira his wife, sold a possession. And he kept back part of the proceeds, his wife also being aware of it, and brought a certain part and laid it at the apostles' feet. But Peter said, 'Ananias, why has Satan filled your heart to lie to the Holy Spirit and keep back part of the price of the land for yourself? While it remained, was it not your own? And after it was sold, was it in your own control? Why have you conceived this thing in your heart? You have not lied to men but to God.'"

There are two points, or maybe even more, that we can pull from these verses. I believe they are vital: one, when we lie to the Holy Spirit it is the same as lying to God; and two, whatever God requests, give it to him, i.e., your talent, time, tithes, offering, etc. So, let's get to know our heavenly Father through our best friend, the One we *ride and live* with, the Holy Spirit. Now let us look for a pastor with a Bible-based church.

CHAPTER SIX — Looking for a Pastor with a Bible-based Church

There is a pastor and church family looking and waiting for you, the gifts that God placed in you, and your ability through the Holy Spirit to help in the vision of the church. You are vital to the body of Christ!

Before we get to the matter, at-hand, providing the information that can lead you to finding a pastor with a Bible-based church, I want you to know that the very first thing you should do is pray. Prayer should always be at the beginning of everything you do, especially when you're seeking direction from God. We're talking about prayer, yes; and you may feel a bit impatient, or you may even have the mindset that you already know about prayer. But believe me, going over this with a new mindset of getting understanding — it will bless your life. Prayer is vital.

Believe it or not, many Christians find excuses to not spend ample time in prayer or to listen to the Holy Spirit. Prayer allows you to bring your *all* to Him, to focus, to acquire an intimacy of oneness with Him. It will also lead you to *not* lean on your thoughts or opinions, outside the Word of God (Proverbs 3:5-6). Check this out:

- Look what the Lord said to Solomon in 1 Kings 3:5 (NIV), "At Gibeon the LORD appeared to Solomon during the night in a dream, and God said, 'Ask for whatever you want me to give you.'" Additionally, he said the same to Solomon in 2 Chronicles 1:7.
- Look what Jesus said in John 14:13 (NASB), "Whatever you ask in My name, that will I do, so that the Father may be glorified in the Son."

Look at this, I like how Matthew 7:7a (NLT) says it regarding asking God, "Keep on asking, and you will receive what you ask for."

Child of God, as stated several times; God does not force us into doing anything. But when we commune with Him, we show our trust is in Him. Prayer is so vital, that in the midst of turmoil, if we allow the Holy Spirit to take control of our lives via our obedience to the Word of God, we will experience what the Bible calls *perfect peace*. It's like having a stillness in Him.

Note that there are more scriptures that you can reference than what is listed here. However, to get understanding let us look at these selected scriptures concerning what the Bible says about prayer:

- 2 Chronicles 7:14 (NIV), "… if my people, who are called by my name, will humble themselves and pray and seek my face and turn from their wicked ways, then I will hear from heaven, and I will forgive their sin and will heal their land."

- Jeremiah 29:12 (NKJV), "Then you will call upon Me and go and pray to Me, and I will listen to you."
- Psalm 17:6 (NLT), "I am praying to you because I know you will answer, O God. Bend down and listen as I pray."
- Luke 18:1 (NLT), "One day Jesus told his disciples a story to show that they should always pray and never give up."
- Ephesians 6:18 (NKJV), "praying always with all prayer and supplication in the Spirit, being watchful to this end with all perseverance and supplication for all the saints"
- Philippians 4:6-7 (NIV), "Do not be anxious about anything, but in every situation, by prayer

and petition, with thanksgiving, present your requests to God. And the peace of God, which transcends all understanding, will guard your hearts and your minds in Christ Jesus."

- Colossians 4:2 (NKJV), "Continue earnestly in prayer, being vigilant in it with thanksgiving."
- 1 Thessalonians 5:17 (NKJV), "Pray without ceasing."

Let me say something here about wanting to give up praying, or giving up in life, period. Because in this life, we will face pressure. There will be no shortage of challenges, purely designed to cause us to run from God, and to give up. Look at Elijah in 1 Kings 19:1-10, he received pressured from Jezebel and he ran to hide. Look at Peter in Luke 22:54-62, when he was pressured, he ran as well. No matter who we are, the level of life we are on or whatever our case may be, feeling the pressure of life is something you and I have in common. But knowing the

Holy Spirit, personally, in your life via the Word of God, He will help you through any life pressure or challenge.

Check this, 2 Corinthians 4:7-9 (NLT) says, "We now have this light shining in our hearts, but we ourselves are like fragile clay jars containing this great treasure. This makes it clear that our great power is from God, not from ourselves. We are pressed on every side by troubles, but we are not crushed. We are perplexed, but not driven to despair. We are hunted down, but never abandoned by God. We get knocked down, but we are not destroyed."

Did you catch that? "We are pressed" on every side by troubles, but not crushed! Do you know why we are not crushed, because we have the Greater One, the presence and power of God, within us through any challenges, situations, and issues that we face here on Earth.

Hallelujah, glory to God!

Let's move on —

Let us talk more on prayer. Because by believing God and His purpose and plan for your life, the Holy Spirit will lead you, and God will add you to that church as in Acts 2:47 (NKJV), where it says, "And the Lord added to the church daily those who were being saved." I believe this. This happened to my wife and me when I retired from the U.S. Navy in 2004. During my military service my family and I traveled a good bit, in and out of the country. We had been to many churches, and down through the years, we had become familiar with several denominations: Baptist, African Methodist Episcopal, Apostolic, etc. I grew up Baptist. My wife grew up Catholic, and I have attended Catholic mass in support of extended family members as well. We have attended nondenominational churches, too. My wife, Janelle, and I have three children. It has been important to us that they have God in their lives. So in 2004, when we settled in the Washington-metropolitan area, the first thing my wife and I did was to pray, not only to find a pastor connected to a Bible-based church, but also we prayed to be unified in our decision. I believe that it is vital for a husband and wife to worship God together in one church. It wasn't too long before He added us to a great Bible-based church, called *Spirit of Faith Christian Center* in Temple Hills, Maryland.

Prior to that time, we searched around the area, and attended several churches that I believe to have had great pastors. But for whatever reason, we were not led to join any of them. God had in mind what He wanted for us, and where He wanted us to be. He also knew what we needed for destiny.

Please know that this is not a knock against, or, as the millenniums like to put it, I am not throwing shade on any pastor and/or church that we visited during our search. We can only believe that they are all doing great work throughout the Kingdom. This is about God specifically providing for our needs, while my wife and I yielded to the Holy Spirit's lead. He knows everything about us, including His plan and purpose for our lives.

While I was on active military duty, there were times when I was stationed overseas, and stationed stateside as well. As I mentioned, we traveled a bit, and because of that there were many instances when we were not able to stay in one church for a long period of time. So that made it impossible to plant roots in one place, but we always made sure that we worshiped together.

Check this out: While you are looking for a church, please do not expect to find a perfect church. During your search, you should be communing with the Holy Spirit to land you in the church that's best for you — a place where you will grow up in God.

When my wife and I found *Spirit of Faith Christian Center*, while waiting to hear confirmation from the Holy Spirit to join; on occasion, we still attended other churches. But also know that we were active in that church, and working to meet the church's needs. We gave our tithes and offerings, we attended weekly Bible studies, and we volunteered in various church events. We wanted to contribute to a body of believers. After a year of attending, we felt assured to join. God provided what we needed, which was the Word of God, teaching us how to live by faith.

Let's move on —

Prayer is key when we need God's direction. The Holy Spirit will lead us, but we must obey where He is taking us.

Let us move on to get understanding. Based on the selected scriptures below, you and I, i.e., the believer, can gain insight on us *being* the church/temple:

- 1 Corinthians 3:9 (NKJV), "For we are God's fellow workers; you are God's field, you are God's building."

- 1 Corinthians 3:16 (NKJV), "Do you not know that you are the temple of God."
- 2 Corinthians 6:16 (NKJV), "For you are the temple of the living God."
- Ephesians 2:21-22 (NKJV), "In whom the whole building, being fitted together, grows into a holy temple in the Lord, (22) In whom you also are being built together for a dwelling place of God in the Spirit."

So as you read, know that each believer is the church. And since this handbook is about helping new Christians, helping those who are seeking Christ, and even nurturing those who are mature in the Word of God, and ever present in getting even more understanding, here's something to know; the Greek word for church is Ekklesia, which means, "called out ones" (*http://www.Biblestudytools.com/lexicons/greek/nas/ekklesia.html*).

And here is something for you to know regarding the phrase “called out”. According to 1 Peter 2:9 (NKJV), “But you [*believer in Christ*] are a chosen generation, a royal priesthood, a holy nation, His own special people, that you may proclaim the praise of Him who *called you out* of darkness into His marvelous light.”

So the church isn’t just a place where you and I go; but the church is every believer in Christ! Christ lives in you as a believer, and this makes you the church. However, we need to go to a church building, and that church should be a Bible-based place of worship. A Bible-based church is a place where believers come together to receive the Word of God from His appointed shepherds, i.e., *pastors*.

Let us move on, looking for a pastor with a Bible-based church.

Let me pause here for a moment to share an essential point. Caution: this may be a little hard to chew or to digest into your thinking. God does not call all pastors, period. And He does not call all pastors to shepherd a Bible-based church. I know that for most of us; we believe every pastor is called by God, and that they are called to lead a Bible-based church, but, beloved, this is just not true.

Child of God, for whatever reason, as long as you choose not to seek the Word of God for your life, you are open game for false teachers, pastors and prophets — to include the impromptu philosophers manning the barbershops, beauty salons, saloons and nightclubs, all those places that harbor public adult activities. And know that there are different seasons for hunting different games. You may have availed yourself to be hunted by any one of them, and to become their prey. That is why the purpose *In All Your Getting, Get Understanding!* is to help anyone to seek God via the Holy Spirit, to renew his or her mind with the Word of God, and to grow in the grace and knowledge of our Lord and Savior Jesus.

To be led astray by anyone teaching lies, and/or the things that God never said or inspired, is not only a waste of your precious time on Earth, but also a serious detour from the promises of God. So that is why we have spent so much time in this chapter regarding prayer. To find a pastor with a Bible-based church, it is time to wake up, pray, read and meditate on the Word, and to believe God by being a doer of what the Word says (James 1:22).

Let's move on —

- Jeremiah 3:15 (NLT) says, "And I (this is God) will give you shepherds (*pastors*) after my own heart, who will guide you with knowledge and understanding."
- Ephesians 4:11 (NLT) says, "Now these are the gifts Christ gave to the church: the apostles, the

> prophets, the evangelists, and the pastors and teachers."

Child of God, let us pause here for a moment to think, while getting understanding. We've touched on this earlier, but it deserves a revisit. I feel strongly about this because I always hear someone saying, "I don't need a pastor," or "I can do church at home." This disturbs my spirit when I come across a person who lacks the understanding about needing to be connected with a body of believers (Hebrews 10:25).

Child of God, what do you think about those statements? Do you think that too? When a person says that he or she does not need a pastor nor does he or she need to attend a Bible-based church that person is simply declining God's gift, and refusing one of the great opportunities to live a better, greater life. This is according to Ephesians 4:11-12 (NLT), where it says, "Now these are the gifts Christ gave to the church: the apostles, the prophets, the evangelists, and the pastors and teachers. Their responsibility is to equip God's people to do his work and build up the church, the body of Christ." So I ask, if you do not have a pastor and if you are not going to a Bible-based church, get there, fast.

Oh, by the way, I am not insensitive. I realize that there are some people who are not able to go to a Bible-based church due to hospitalization, bedrest, or being subject to a doctor's orders or a confinement due to other reasons. Perhaps someone has physical challenges. Even still, there are men, women and children suffering in war zones, worldwide. There could be many reasons to physically prevent someone from attending inside the doors of a church. There could be many challenges in the body, even while we still believe they are healed (Isaiah 53:5). However, for those who are able to physically attend and join a Bible-based church, look what Hebrews 10:25 (TLB) says, "Let us not neglect our church meetings, as some people do, but encourage and warn each other, especially now that the day of his [Jesus] coming back again is drawing near."

Child of God, what about the person who says, "I have a personal relationship with Jesus because He knows my heart." Please understand that anyone who is not a member and/or committed to God's church, runs the risk of missing out on a full measure of spiritual and physical activities, love and nurturing that comprises the unity of a church family.

To the doubters, who may have heard negative things about the church, or even experienced negativity, perhaps, in one particular church or another, I would strongly suggest that you do not give up your search to find a Bible-based church. God has one for you.

As children of God, within our churches, we need everyone's gifts, talents, abilities, love, strength, encouragement, laughter, and fellowship in Christ Jesus.

While you're looking for a pastor with a Bible-based church, we have acknowledged that this may take some time, but don't take too long. Time is of the essence. You see, everyone has different ideals, opinions, and other things he or she would like to see in a pastor with a Bible-based church. However, I believe it is safe to say that nearly everyone wants to see, and know, that his or her pastor has love for every congregant. And that their pastor welcomes everyone into the house of the Lord. Additionally, everyone wants a pastor who can effectively teach, while being consistently transparent.

Also know that some folks looking for a church have preferences as to whether or not they would feel at home in a mega church or in a smaller, hometown church. For some it is important if the church is involved in outreach efforts in the community, especially to the less fortunate, or if it operates outreach efforts overseas as well.

I asked a few precious people of God what their preferences were regarding what they'd like to see in a pastor and/or a church — as a church member. Check out their responses (last names have been omitted):

Joan from Orange, NJ said that what she looks for in a pastor, "is that he's extroverted."

Richie from Greensboro, NC said that what he would like to see in a pastor, "is a commitment to the community, and [his pastor must] have a spiritual presence as well as be a compassionate person [to] teach, which makes it easier to understand the Word in layman terms."

Cynthia from Maplewood, NJ said that her pastor must be, "is a spiritual leader/father, someone who God anointed to deliver His Word."

Alfred from Jacksonville, FL looks for a pastor who, "teaches scripture. I believe he or she should always teach and preach from the Bible, the Word of God, and not in his or her own interpretation."

Cebronica, my daughter, from Indiana, IN said, "When I am selecting a pastor, I look for someone who focuses on educating and strengthening my biblical knowledge. I really enjoy pastors who provide historical context to their sermons in addition to scriptures and parables. Providing that context shows that they have done their research and are sincerely studying what was happening in the world when the text was being written. To me, that provides me with deeper insight on why we are who we are, and how we can become more Christ-like when applying it to our lives in present time."

Terri from Jersey City, NJ said, "I look for a pastor who displays faith, acknowledges the importance of the Holy Spirit, one who rightly divides the Word of God, adheres to biblical principles, and has a heart and love for the people."

El Chere from Atlanta, GA said that she, "would like her pastor to be a true man of God, living in true Holiness."

James from Bowie, MD said, "I want a pastor who's living what he or she is teaching from the pulpit and displaying God's unconditional love for the people."

Lisa from Jacksonville, FL said, "I want a pastor who knows the Word, who is truly Bible-based and can turn the Bible into understandable life lessons."

As you can read, everyone owns different preferences for what he or she wants to see in a pastor with a Bible-based church. Hey, when a person looks forward to buying a house, he or she researches the real estate market before coming to a decision. Why? Because it's wise to do one's research, and even to take one's time — but not too much time. The house a person settles on will be a part of that person's life, and their family's life for an infinite amount of time. Their house will comfort them, protect them from storms, no matter the season, and be the place to welcome others. So you don't just want to settle on any house. They want to be wise, not foolish. Look at Matthew 7:24-27 (NKJV), "Therefore whoever hears these sayings of Mine, and does them, I will liken him to a wise man who built his house on the rock: and the rain descended, the floods came, and the winds blew and beat on that house; and it did not fall, for it was found on the rock. But everyone who hears these sayings of Mine, and does not do them, will be like a foolish man who built his house on the sand: and the rain descended, the floods came, and the winds blew and beat on that house; and it fell. And great was its fall."

Child of God, whatever you are doing to include looking for a pastor with a Bible-based church, you want to be wise, not foolish.

Well, I believe that you want to find a pastor who relishes in helping people to excel in every area of life, as he or she also shepherds them by way of the Word of God. This is important because it is your life that you are placing under a pastor's leadership. With that said, you need a pastor who is not afraid to correct you when you veer astray, and who will still love-up on you after his or her correction.

So, if you are a new Christian or someone who has been walking with the Lord for some time and realized that you need a church, here are things you can consider:

1. On the Internet — you can research churches and explore what they have to offer:

- You can read about the pastor.
- Find out a church's beliefs.
- Discover the impact churches are doing locally and globally.

- Do they have a children's Sunday school/church? It is important on many levels that children grow up in church.
- Do they have something for teens? Teens need to express Jesus at their level as well.
- Do they have a Young Adult Service? We need to prepare young adults for the spiritual challenges that will come, and the faith questions they will face. By having this service, it will assist young adults to grow up in a bona fide relationship with Jesus.

Note: most people will join their family's church because of tradition. I caution you about that because a few traditions can tend to cause a person to become stuck and/or stagnant without even knowing it. If that is the case, it is possible that he or she is not growing in the Word of God. Also it's possible for a tradition to cause a person to lose his or her focus when the Word is being taught. Example: There are believers who absolutely must sit on the same church pew. They will even ask a visitor to move if that visitor should sit in their perceived space. Such an action can cause adverse attitudes about the church. A leader in the church, who insists on sitting on the front pew, a place of importance, because he or she was told that this was the tradition of all church leaders, demonstrates the lack of understanding about servanthood. It's not wrong to sit on the front row, however, leaders of the church should never allow it to become a blind tradition — especially when it unwelcomes visitors. Remember, every Christian has the Holy Spirit living within them to guide them. It is also the responsibility of every Christian to obey Him, to follow Him, and to grow up in the ways of God.

With that said, please know that all traditions are not bad. In fact, some traditions can even bring order and purpose to the church services, rendered. But you want to make sure that the traditions you have come to follow are fruitful, that the seekers of the Word can bite and benefit. Church traditions should bear fruit.

2. Word of mouth — ask around and listen to what people are saying about their church.

3. Visit a church — at least three-to-four times, along with attending:

- Bible studies
- prayer meetings
- taking part in what a church is doing throughout its communities.

Additionally, find out how a church views scripture because interpretations may vary. It is your responsibility, as a believer, to study, read and examine the words you hear coming across any pulpit and/or from whomever (Acts 17:11). Don't just take my word, the pastor, the teacher's word, or whomever is giving instruction from the Word. As a student under the guidance of the Holy Spirit, search the scripture for yourself. Follow the instruction according to 2 Timothy 2:15 (NKJV), where it says, "Be diligent to present yourself approved to God, a worker who does not need to be ashamed, rightly dividing the word of truth." Wow, the study of God's Word is crucial to spiritual growth. Therefore, don't be lazy regarding anything that enhances your life via the Word of God. Study!

Child of God, you want to find out about the church you are considering to join. Does it believe the Bible, according to 2 Timothy 3:16 (NKJV), where it says, "All Scripture is given by inspiration of God, and is profitable for doctrine, for reproof, for correction, for instruction in righteousness …"? Besides that, know this, according to

2 Peter 1:20-21 (NKJV), "… knowing this first, that no prophecy of Scripture is of any private interpretation, for prophecy never came by the will of man, but holy men of God spoke as they were moved by the Holy Spirit."

In all you're getting, gain understanding about who you are in Him, what you have in Him, and what you can do through Him. Additionally, keep in mind that *you* are the church, looking for a pastor with a Bible-based church. Once you find this church, it can enhance your life journey, which is not just for this life. This is most important for understanding your eternity with your heavenly Father.

Once you've found your church home, you should be willing to come under the authority of Scripture with joy. This is your life. You have one shot, here, on Earth. Allow God to lead you to your place of worship (Deuteronomy 12:11).

Oh, by the way, let me add this; we need pastors after the heart of God to help God's people to discover and to stir up their gifts. We need them to teach what spiritual gifts are, and how you and I can better serve the advancement of the Kingdom of God.

Now go and find your pastor with a Bible-based church.

CHAPTER SEVEN — Renew Your Mind, Part I

We have to reprogram what has been programmed via the Word of God, to think like Christ.

When I first accepted Jesus as my Lord and Savior, no one ever explained to me about renewing my mind. I thought that being saved was it, and that everything else would just fall into place. It was like equating my salvation with a magic trick. I had accepted Jesus Christ as my Savior, strong and bold, and poof — all my problems would vanish. After all, wasn't I told to just come to God and He will fix it? Well, that's true. But how come, I was still battling one problem after another, still feeling overwhelmed, and still feeling defeated by life?

During my formative years, I had heard all about Jesus, and I even had some of His truth under my belt.

But I was like a baby, still surviving on formula. And, perhaps, I wasn't even ready for all that He had for me (1Corinthians 3:2). You see, what Jesus has done for us all, throughout the universe, is to die for us and rise again; so that we will have the opportunity to live throughout eternity with our God the Father and worship Him on Earth. However, as you may already know, in order to have eternal life, one must first receive Jesus as your Lord and Savior. Prayerfully, you have already done this.

Well, as you've read, I had done that. But, still my problems and challenges persisted. Like many people who have grown up in the church, I initially gave my life to Christ as a young child. I was at the tender age of eight. But as an adult, I believe that it was an unction in my spirit that caused me to desire to have a better understanding about God. I know, now, that such a desire was inspired by the Holy Spirit.

In my early thirties, I was a sailor stationed in South Carolina, but assigned to a Navy Information Technician (IT) School in San Diego. While in San Diego, my wife and three young children were safely situated in Navy Housing located in Goose Creek, South Carolina. That not only left me free to handle my studies by day, but also it left me free to delve into my demons by night. For me, that demon was drinking. And let me add that during this time, I was always living from paycheck-to-paycheck, and not wanting to pay some of my bills, which caused debt. After all, though I made sure that my family did not lack, I needed whatever was left over to party. I lived in the barracks, and another young sailor, whom I will never forget, lived a couple doors down. I first noticed him because he was an immediate source of irritation to me.

Whenever he was not in uniform, he adorned a ball cap that brandished the name, Jesus, on the front. It got on my nerves, especially if I ran into him, in the midst of me being intoxicated. So my first thought, naturally, was to stay away from him. However, whenever he saw me his smile was inviting, and void of judgment. What I will say about that sailor today, who later came to be my brother-in-Christ, is that he, and his ball cap, ended up being a vehicle that led me to return to Christ.

At the age of eight years old, I had been saved by Christ, but it was not until I had reached my thirties … that' s when I was ready to learn about, and accept the life that I have in Christ. Please understand that during this time there were many instances where I felt emotionally stuck in my life. Frustration, and unanswered questions plagued me, and there was a measure of time when I just wanted to give up — on my family — and just move on with my life. Why? Because of misinformation about living for God, coupled with my negative thoughts that continuously led me to make bad decisions. In short, though I had accepted Christ, I was still living a defeated life. I lacked understanding to move forward in the victory through the Death, Burial and Resurrection of Jesus. Look what 1 Corinthians 15:57 (NLT) says, "But thank God! He gives us victory over sin and death through our Lord Jesus Christ."

Child of God, I'm not blaming anyone for the missteps that happened to me during my earlier adulthood walk with God. I take full responsibility for the negative decisions and actions that could have been prevented. I do feel that if I had come across the understanding of renewing my mind, then some of my prior negative outcomes may not have occurred. This also goes hand-in-hand with the measure of faith residing in me from God. Remember, we talked about the measure of faith in Chapter Four.

I believe there are Christians, today, who either don't know about the concept of renewing their minds and/or they have yet to make an intentional move to renew their minds in Christ. For some, they are filling up their lives with false hopes, void of action. Or they are sitting in front of the television confusing reality with make-believe, waiting for the Holy Spirit to swoop in like Superman and magically scoop away their problems and challenges. Others are hanging out and socializing at coffee shops or hanging out in front of the neighborhood store versed in meaningless conversations. Some have fallen into the stagnate routines, day-in and day-out, unable or unwilling to do something new. Please understand that I'm not throwing shade on having a social life or needing down time. And of course, most people are hardworking, striving to take care of their families and to pay their bills on time. But the problem comes in when someone is asked or invited to visit a

Bible-based church to attend a service or a Bible study — a place where they *may* have an opportunity to learn about the renewing of the mind to live a better life in Christ, and that person will tell you that they are too busy. They go to work, stop at the supermarket or the mall; then wrap up their evening posting on social media. But there is no time to study the Word of God.

Check this out: I know this because this is another thing to which I fell prey. And I believe that others have experienced this as well. I treated myself to things that I either didn't need or soon lost interest in. Often many of us fall into that trap because we are trying to impress others or trying to fill the spiritual void in our lives. Then we go to church on Sunday, and say, "God knows my heart," and use that reasoning to not render tithes and offerings to the Lord. Why? Because those actions reflect a mind that needs to be renewed via the Word of God.

Child of God, what's just been mentioned, occurring in the lives of precious people, to include me, most likely has gone on for years. Such behaviors and thinking, especially in abundance, is not likely to be conducive to positive life-changing results — such as accomplishing the dreams, goals and the godly desires of one's heart via the victory of Jesus. However, today, as you read this, your mind is being renewed by faith.

In the year of 1972, the *United Negro College Fund* came up with a very effective slogan. It read, "A mind is a terrible thing to waste." Please allow me to add that a mind, and a soul is a terrible thing to waste.

This is what the apostle Paul said according to Romans 12:2 (NIV), "Do not conform to the pattern of this world, but be transformed by the renewing of your mind. Then you will be able test and approve what God's will is — His good, pleasing and perfect will [for your life]." This is vital for the Christian to prevent the world from shaping his or her mind causing him or her to miss out on the benefits of God. So what does it mean to renew your mind?

To renew your mind means to bring your mind into an agreement with the mind of Christ via the Word of God. It means to align your attitude, your lifestyle, your actions, and your viewpoints (e.g., your ideals, values) with what the Word of God says.

Child of God, renewing your mind is a moment-to-moment, day-to-day, month-to-month and year-to-year lifelong journey.

Knowing how important this is for every believer, here are two more translations according to Romans 12:2. By faith, this will increase your understanding:

- Romans 12:2 (NCV) "Do not be shaped by this world; instead be changed within by a new way of thinking. Then you will be able to decide what

God wants for you; you will know what is good and pleasing to him and what is perfect."

- Romans 12:2 (Phillips) "Don't let the world around you squeeze you into its own mould, but let God re-mould your minds from within, so that you may prove in practice that the plan of God for you is good, meets all his demands and moves toward the goal of true maturity."

Renewing your mind allows your transformation. This is done by faith with the help of the Holy Spirit. You will find yourself living more and more like Christ on Earth. Look how 2 Corinthians 3:18b (TLB) put it, "… And as the Spirit of the Lord works within us, we become more and more like him."

As the Holy Spirit is at work in our lives we are by faith reflecting on the things of God in every area of life. This is through the process of renewing our mind that allows the transformation by faith to be who God called us to be, to do what He asked of us, and have the experience of the God-filled life Jesus came to give (John 10:10) on Earth.

Every believer has a choice in this. Making such a decision is not forced upon you by God. Should you make this decision, and take this tangible step, I believe you will embark on a life-fulfilling course that will reflect godly right-thinking. And as you do that, I also believe this is another area in the process of renewing your mind.

If you read my devotional collection, titled *Any Day Devotion*, which is a Bible-based resource for daily living, it addresses this process, and it can help you along with the guided life of the Holy Spirit. It's designed to encourage you and enhance your growing personal relationship with Christ. *Any Day Devotion* is just as the title proclaims, it is applicable on any given day of your life. Should you explore these devotional reads, you will discover an encouragement, titled, *How's Your Thinking,*

It is a tool to check your day-to-day thinking and to ensure you are on the right course of life regarding how you think.

Thinking is a major part of everything we do in life. Our thinking should reflect the ability God has given us to help better the world by solving problems, cures, poverty, etc. If we do not think right, how can we effectively react to any given situation, problem, or challenge? Thinking determines where we are in the present, and where we are headed.

I know how important it is to have right-thinking, and actions. Wrong thinking can lead to wrong actions with, sometimes, catastrophic consequences. In my younger days, a friend and I were desperate for money. And all we could think of was that we needed money, right then. Well, we were hashing out our right-now dilemma, while sitting in front of a convenience store. The longer we talked, and the more intoxicated we grew, the more enticing the convenience store became to us. Before we knew it, we were lusting after money that was not ours. Our ill-gotten thoughts were running rampant. All of a sudden, one of us said to the other, “Let’s rob the place.” And, boom, we were in total agreement.

Wasn’t that a crazy way to think? Thank God, it was a thought upon which we did not act. I know, today, that it was the Holy Spirit within me — even though I wasn’t fully aware of His presence. Right then, in the moment, He called up in me the consequences of wrong thinking that could have led to criminal activity, and having to pay the price for it, i.e., prison, separation from family, and even losing my livelihood.

Mmm … it is possible for desperate thinking to bring unwanted results. Right here and now, you can benefit from my close call. Renewing your mind will cause you to cast down negative thoughts before they hatch into ungodly desires and negative actions. Everything we do derives from everything we think. That's why we need to examine our thinking before reacting in all cases.

Once a person is converted into being born-again, his or her thinking should begin to center on the life of God that is within them versus centering on outside-world influences.

Romans 5:12 clearly tell us that through Adam, sin entered the world. You and I inherited sin because of what Adam had done in the Garden of Eden [Genesis 2:15-17 & 3:6]. Our minds and thinking are worldly because of our flesh being of sin-nature. According to Romans 8:7 (NASB) it says, "… because the mind set on the flesh is hostile toward God; for it does not subject itself to the law of God, for it is not even able to do so."

This is important, and key in Christ, according to 1 Corinthians 2:14-16 (NKJV), "But the natural man does not receive the things of the Spirit of God, for they are foolishness to him; nor can he know them, because they are spiritually discerned. But he who is spiritual [born-again] judges all things, yet himself is rightly judged by no one. For *'who has known the mind of the Lord that he may instruct Him?'* But we [born-again] have the mind of Christ." In addition, Philippians 2:5 (NKJV) says, "Let this mind be in you which was also in Christ Jesus."

Every believer has the mind of Christ; however, sadly, that does not mean that every believer is allowing their mind to think like Christ. Hence, when I was in the midst of thinking about robbing that convenience store, I had the mind of Christ, but was not utilizing the benefits of it. I had not made an intentional move to renew my mind. And to do that, as it was mentioned earlier, every believer must spend time in the Word of God, and allow that Word to become saturated in his or her daily life. Our thinking should involve meditating on what the Word of God says while no longer allowing the world's ways to fashion our thinking.

To help believers think and align themselves with the Word of God, and to know what to meditate on, apostle Paul gives us great advice. According to Philippians 4:8-9 (NKJV), "Finally, brethren, whatever things are true, whatever things are noble, whatever things are just, whatever things are pure, whatever things are lovely, whatever things are of good report, if there is any virtue and if there is anything praiseworthy — meditate on these things. The things which you learned and received and heard and saw in me, these do, and the God of peace will be with you."

Thank God for apostle Paul giving us examples to follow in these eight things that reflect God's peace and shows us what to think on: (1) *whatever things are* true — this means real and genuine, and no lies attached. (2) *Whatever things are noble* — this means honorable and worthy. And highly respected. (3) *Whatever things are just* — this means right and righteous like God's goodness and His love for us. It also means that we should reflect that same love toward others. It shows up in our actions and behaviors toward others. (4) *Whatever things are pure* — this means morally clean, spotless, and stainless. Every believer should work to prevent his or her mind from being contaminated by ungodly thoughts. Anything other than that we must cast it down (5) *Whatever things are lovely* — this translates into pleasing, kind, and gracious; additionally you can work to motivate love and kindness in others to reflect heaven's atmosphere on Earth. (6) *Whatever things are of a good report* — this means a report of commendable things in your daily life that can add to the faith-life of someone else, for example, your testimony. However, keep in mind that actions and thoughts that can negatively affect yourself and others would not be thought of as good reports. (7) *If there be any virtue* — this means excellence, (8) *and if there be any praiseworthy* —

meditate on these things — this translates into any of our thoughts.

What apostle Paul mentioned regarding those eight things was meant to help us as believers to not be anxious for anything, but to have peace even in the midst of every challenge in life (Philippians 4:6-7) and to be set on the right course of our thinking.

However, let me be direct; thinking positively, working to align one's self with the Word of God, does not mean that all life challenges will stop. In contrast, however, by faith with the Holy Spirit help and the Word of God, we are able to handle those challenges through the finished work of Jesus. This causes us to maintain our victory position on Earth.

Look at Proverbs 23:7 (NKJV) which says, "For as he thinks in his heart, so is he." I believe that is one of the most powerful functions of the human body is the function to think. However, it depends on what you choose to think about and/or how you center your thoughts that can determine the outcomes throughout your life journey. Our thoughts can do one of two things: 1. They can help maintain our victory position in Christ or 2. They can relegate us to living a defeated life of lack.

Most of what occurs in our lives happens because of the way you and I think. Wrong thinking outside of the Word of God produces worry. Look at Isaiah 26:3 (NKJV), "You will keep him in perfect peace, whose mind is stayed on You." Wow, we don't have perfect peace because our minds are not stayed on God. The Old Testament's Hebrew word for 'mind' in this selected scripture refers to that part of our imagination that causes us to lose our peace. Our imagination runs untamed and can sometimes harbor all kinds of wrong thinking/negative thoughts. Additionally, wrong thinking outside of the Word produces incorrect emotions, reactions, behavior and discontent!

What you think about reflects your actions. Your actions reflect your consequences. Your decisions reflect the plus or minus costs of your life, and where you stand, today. Furthermore, you're thinking reflects how you see yourself in every life situation, challenge, and problem. For example: Do you see yourself as a winner or a loser? How you see yourself should have nothing to do with how others see you — or what others say about you. Love yourself, and place in the highest esteem all the things that God says and thinks about you — live accordingly.

Let's move on —

Look at Proverbs 26:11(NLT). Now this is strong, but it should move us to check our thinking and actions. Here's what this scripture says, "As a dog returns to its vomit, so a fool repeats his foolishness." Why would anyone, to include you and me, continue to do those foolishness things that leave us stuck in life with the same negative/lack results. Why would anyone want the same result of being broke by spending and living beyond his or her means? Why would an inmate get released, and then end up back into prison as a repeat offender, continuously? Why would anyone keep speeding down the same street with traffic warnings declaring the safety speed limit as twenty-five miles, even in the face of receiving multiple speeding tickets? Well, perhaps these rounds of repetitive actions signal that we are in need of a new mindset. We need to renew our minds.

The Word of God is an important key to moving forward in direction of your dreams, goals, godly desires, and destiny. You can hear God's voice, down in your spirit, as you meditate on what it says. Joshua 1:8 (NASB) says, "This book of the law shall not depart from your mouth, but you shall meditate on it day and night, so that you may be careful to do according to all that is written in it; for then you will make your way prosperous, and then you will have success."

Wow, go ahead, read that again! Stay continuous in the Word, especially during those challenges, situations, and issues. Being a witness for God via our living and sharing the Word is a result of meditating on the Word. This shows our obedience. And as with Joshua, you and I, too, will be prosperous and have success. Glory to God!

Child of God, God is not in a box or locked up in man's traditions. Tight thinking inside the box causes us to block and/or slow down the manifestations of our goals, godly desires that are in our hearts, and those dreams that we want to become a reality. Think outside the box, not belonging to the world or to other people's ungodly opinions. In the matter of moving forward, remember my pastor's quote mentioned in Chapter Five. Plainly and poignantly, Dr. Freeman says, "Divorce yourself from the opinions of others." Wise advice that he also shares with the congregation.

That is what the disciple, Peter, had done according to Matthew 14:22-29. Peter and the other disciples were in a boat being tossed by the waves. He acknowledged that they were all afraid. However, Peter did not allow their tight-box thinking (i.e., fears, negative opinions, and foolish talk) to stop him walking toward Jesus.

As Jesus was walking on the water toward the disciples, He said, "be of good cheer! It is I; do not be afraid." Peter answered Him and said, "Lord, if it is You, command me to come to You on the water." So He said, "come." Peter's actions, thinking and faith were all operating outside of the box. Note that outside-the-box was where Jesus stood.

Here is a nugget that challenges us throughout our life journey, especially when it comes to living in a suffocating box, which is generally the home of negative people, negative thoughts and stalemate traditions. I challenge you to free yourself from those who do not want to have better than what they have today, meaning those living minus the expectation of receiving more from God. Why? Because we all have one shot on Earth. You want to enjoy, rejoice and be glad in everything (Psalm 118:24) that the Lord has already given!

So the Holy Spirit via my conscience (Romans 9:1) said something that I remembered (John 14:26) and obeyed. This stopped me in the way of my negative thought, and *almost* action, of robbing a convenience store. He gave me the chance, and the choice, to seek the renewing of my mind. During my years of getting understanding, I have intentionally moved toward the positive, and positive people. Needless to say, I've lost touch with my former *almost* partner-in-crime.

Here's more about Peter and the other disciples in the boat. Yes, Peter stepped out of the boat, but in doing so, he also had to step out of the boat of his five senses: sight, hearing, taste, smell, and touch. Now all of these senses are vital to all of us. And our senses have been placed inside of us by God. However, as we learn to manage them with wisdom and understanding, faith still moves us forward. Peter had to manage his human senses to get to Jesus. Also note that the operative word, here, is faith. If we do not invoke our faith, as Peter did, our human senses could hinder us and keep us stagnate in life.

Just think and imagine the sight of those waves, and Peter — or you — hearing the frightened and negative opinions about what he should not do. Imagine Peter tasting the bitterness of the water, having it smashing against his face, perhaps, smelling vomit, and feeling the hands of others pulling him to their perceived points of safety. Although, each one of our senses has a distinct purpose, there are times when we must push beyond any one of them to move forward in the things of God. And that takes faith.

Child of God, remember that our five senses deal with the natural world, while our faith works in the supernatural/spiritual realm. But it is our faith that brings to us everything we are believing God for — into the natural.

Let us pray, here, concerning those senses because if we are not mindful, they can cause us unnecessary challenges and mismanagement:

Thank you Heavenly Father for the Holy Spirit who is our guide and helper throughout life on Earth. Thank you that by faith we are not solely moved by sight, hearing, taste, smell and touch. Although they are an important part of life, we are only moved by Your voice via the Holy Spirit, and the Word of God by faith. Father, we refuse to be moved to follow strangers (John 10:27). However, by faith we choose, "Your word [*that*] *is* a lamp to my feet and a light to my path (Psalm 119:105 NKJV), in Jesus' name, Amen!

This brings me to say that faith is important for every believer to live by. Having faith pleases God. We discussed this in Chapter Four, *The Measure of Faith.*

Peter gave us an example of thinking and doing things outside the box, which was by faith, to help us understand that anyone in Christ can reach higher, go farther and wider with the Lord each day.

I lived this, again, when I returned to school to receive my bachelor's degree from the University of Maryland University College (UMUC). I walked across that stage in May of 2016. Although it took me more than twenty years to receive my degree, I still praised God. And, I'm still praising Him for helping me to endure all the life challenges that came with my academic journey. In addition to my studies, I was still the head of my household. I was still the father of my three children, and the husband to my wife. I still held down a fulltime job. I was an adult learner, working hard to keep up with my younger fellow classmates, and I wanted to achieve, not just maintain. Sleep was a rare commodity. And as if all that wasn't enough, it was most important to me that I nourished the Christian walk of my precious three children. I wanted my family to always see the God in me, no matter the challenge. Believe me when I share with you that there wasn't any part of this that came easy.

But to accomplish it all, I had to move past the opinions of others that spouted how I was not college material. I did not allow my emotions to get the better of me because they often touted my lack of confidence and doubt that I could succeed. This happened to me even while I knew that what I was trying to accomplish had the power to impact my family, generations-to-come. I was working to break a cycle. And I did not allow the years of negative occurrences that I had witnessed taking place in my extended family or during my military career, or even in my community to derail me from my goal. Please note that I mean no disrespect to the legacy and love given to me by generations of my family and/or the legacy and love given to you by your family. It's just that for us all, challenges have abounded. In multiple instances, many may lack the courage to pursue a formal education because of what others may have said about them, such as "you'll never 'mount up to anything good in life."

So, let us step out of the boat to accomplish all the godly things that God has placed in us to do. Let us renew our minds to enhance our walk with God.

CHAPTER EIGHT— Renew Your Mind, Part II

As you continue to renew your mind do not allow the enemy, who is a liar according to John 8:44, to get you off track. The enemy will use people to discourage you by saying; "You are still the same. There is nothing in you or about you that has changed for the good." He is cunning and will challenge you by twisting the Word of God (Genesis 3:1).

Child of God, by renewing your mind, you will learn about the tricks of Satan. According to Matthew 4:1-11(NKJV), Satan tried to temp Jesus to do several things as well as test His identity. This is what he said in verses three and four, "If you are the Son of God command that these stones become bread. But Jesus answered and said, 'It is written, man shall not live by bread alone, but by every word that proceeds from the mouth of God.'"

You and I know that Jesus is the Son of God; however, Satan is the tempter, liar, enemy, and an accuser of God's people. Not only does Satan want us to doubt the fact that Jesus Christ is the Son of God, but also he wants you and I to doubt who we are in Christ. Each time Satan says something to your mind, cast it down by speaking the Word of God. Do not allow his negative thoughts and untruths to nest in your mind. God wills for His children is to know the Word of truth. If we ever hear the word of error, it is not of God.

During my early walk with God, as an adult, no one ever told me about the seriousness of controlling the negative thoughts that would run through my mind, unchecked. And if I was able to identity a negative thought as well as the mind-battles it caused; I did not know who, exactly, could help me. I needed to know how to apply the Word to help me understand and learn how to control those thoughts. Taking control over our thoughts is crucial for us all to move forward.

It is necessary to understand that when a thought enters your mind, you must check it against the Word of God. Every thought is not a bad thought. Remember, be slow to action, but quick to discern from the Holy Spirit. I know that this is challenging. But hold on!

Check this out: During the end of my Navy tour in Yokosuka Japan, I had challenges sleeping at night. I attributed it to the likes of racing and negative thoughts (i.e., death, unachieved goals, worry over negative events that had not happened, etc.). Every night, I fought insomnia.

This went on for weeks, so I decided to see a doctor. Well, I visited the doctor, and he prescribed a medication for me to try. Sadly, it did not work for me, and my restless and sleepless nights persisted.

Mmm … that said, please allow me to pause right here to issue a *Spiritual Public Service Announcement*: There is nothing wrong or ungodly about seeking medical attention and/or a physician when it comes to your health. Also, there is nothing ungodly about following the doctor's orders when it comes to medical procedures or taking medication. Respectfully, all (and/or any) of this should be metered, individually. Beloved, I'm sharing my personal testimony out of love, and because I want to encourage you. I am not giving you medical advice. Respectfully, this is the end of our *Spiritual Public Service Announcement*. Now, back to our *Regular Christian Programming to Get Understanding*.

Well, my doctor informed me that everything will not help everyone. Sometimes medication works, sometimes it doesn't — according to a patient's individual basis. For me, my sleepless nights persisted. I tried to exercise at the gym until I grew tired and felt ready to go to sleep. But that did not work. I researched the Internet, and found what I thought was some good information on chemical imbalances. The corresponding remedies I read about, helped me for a short time, which made me happy. However, a full and restful night's sleep still eluded me. Without adequate sleep, I could not focus during my workdays. I felt at the mercy of these racing negative thoughts running rampant in my mind.

One day everything changed. God sent me an ever-present help. It came in the form of someone making me aware of Proverbs 3:24 (NIV). It states, "When you lie down, you will not be afraid; when you lie down, your sleep will be sweet." *Wow*, I thought to myself, *God wants us to have sweet sleep. So how do I get to this?*

Like any negative thought that does not align itself with the Word of God, it must be cast down by speaking God's Word. Look at 2 Corinthians 10:4-5, "For the weapons of our warfare are not carnal but mighty in God for pulling down strongholds, casting down arguments and every high thing that exalts itself against the knowledge of God, bringing every thought into captivity to the obedience of Christ …"

Child of God, for me, being pointed to that Word of scripture eventually led me to commandeer sweet sleep. As best as I can recall it, this was the beginning of acknowledging the strongholds of negative thinking, and the riches of renewing one's mind. So today, whenever I am challenged by negative thoughts, I know to cast them down. I get out of bed, go to another room, and reach for my Bible. Praying and reading God-inspired scripture relaxes my mind, especially from the day's hectic events and thoughts. Please let me take a minute to stress that this is something that is in your power to do — without the aid of your pastor. Read your Bible. Increase your personal relationship with God, so that you will be in-tune to His Word.

Now, let's not get this thing twisted, and think that the enemy will stop trying to pursue you with negative thoughts. But remember that no matter what Satan tries to do, he is a lair. The Bible declares that God cannot lie (Numbers 23:19 and Titus 1:2). The Word of God is true (Psalm 119:160). So by faith, cast down every thought that is not of God with the Word of God. And remember Jesus' example in the wilderness, found in Matthew 4:3-4 (NKJV), where He used the Word against Satan by saying, "It is written, Man shall not live by bread alone, but by every word that proceeds from the mouth of God." That is how we are to cast down those crazy, wrong, negative, sinful and racing thoughts — we speak the words of Jesus.

Additionally, and we covered this in earlier chapters, know that speaking and reading the Word of God encompasses the act of believing it, confessing it, and being a doer of the Word of God.

Child of God, do not fall prey to negative thoughts and unfounded negative opinions that others say about you. Always lean on what God's Word says about you. God's Word takes weight over what anybody else says. Prayerfully, the following selected scriptures will enhance your ability to renew your mind, to cast down negative thoughts, and these scriptures will help you meditate on the wealth of God's Word:

- 2 Timothy 1:7 (NKJV) says, "For God has not given us a spirit of fear, but of power and of love and of a sound mind."
- 1 Peter 1:13 (NLT) says, "So think clearly and exercise self-control. Look forward to the gracious salvation that will come to you when Jesus Christ revealed to the world."
- Ephesians 4:23 (NKJV) says, "… and be renewed in the spirit of your mind ..."

- Hebrews 10:16 (NKJV) says "This is the covenant that I will make with them after those days, say the Lord: I will put My laws into their hearts, and in their minds I will write them …"
- Philippians 4:7 (NKJV) says, "… and the peace of God, which surpasses all understanding, will guard your hearts and minds through Christ Jesus."
- Romans 8:5-7 (NKJV) says, "For those who live according to the flesh set their minds on the things of the flesh, but those who live according to the Spirit, the things of the Spirit. For to be carnally minded is death, but to be spiritually minded is life and peace. Because the carnal mind is enmity against God: for it is not subject to the law of God, nor indeed can be."

Now meditate by seeing and knowing who you are in Christ via these selected scriptures:

- Because of accepting Jesus, you are a member of Christ's Body (1 Corinthians 12:27)
- You are born-again (1 Peter 1:23)
- You are a new creation (2 Corinthians 5:17)
- You are delivered (Colossians 1:13)
- You are redeemed from the curse of the Law (Galatians 3:13)
- You are forgiven (Ephesians 1:7; Colossians 1:14)
- You are adopted as his child (Ephesians 1:5)
- You are in Him (Ephesians 1:7; 1 Corinthians 1:30)
- You are God's child (John 1:12)
- You are precious and honored by God (Isaiah 43:4)
- You belong to God (1 Corinthians 6:20)

- You are God's very own and protected (John 10:28)
- You are blessed in the heavenly realms with every spiritual blessing (Ephesians 1:3)
- You are chosen before the creation of the world (Ephesians 1:4, 11)
- You have redemption (Ephesians 1:8)
- You have purpose (Ephesians 1:9 & 3:11)
- You are God's workmanship (Ephesians 2:10)
- You are a holy temple (Ephesians 2:21; 1 Corinthians 6:19)
- You are God's very own possession/special people (1 Peter 2:9)
- You are a dwelling for the Holy Spirit (Ephesians 2:22)
- You share in the promise of Christ Jesus (Ephesians 3:6)

- You are not helpless in any situation or through any challenge (Philippians 4:13)
- You have overcome (1 John 4:4)
- God's power works through you (Ephesians 3:7&20, Ephesians 6:10)
- You are victorious (1 John 5:4, 1 Corinthians 15:57)
- I can have a new attitude and a new lifestyle (Ephesians 4:21-32)
- I can be kind and compassionate to others (Ephesians 4:32)
- I can forgive others (Ephesians 4:32)
- I am victorious (1 John 5:4)
- I can love by faith (John 3:16, 1 Corinthians 13:8a, Galatians 5:13-13, Hebrews 13:1, James 2:8, 1 John 4:10-11 etc.)

Beloved, let's not get it twisted. Although we have a new spirit, our souls and our minds are still un-renewed. This is why we, even so, commit sin actions; possibly react negatively and worldly to life setbacks, disappointments, etc. Child of God, you and I cannot control the circumstances or events of our life. However, how we react to them in life reveals a lot about our minds. So let's bring our minds into alignment with our spirits; and renew them with the Word of God.

CHAPTER NINE — Distractions

What is a distraction?

On www.dictionary.com, one can find a definition for the word *distraction*. It states: *that which distracts, divides the attention, or prevents concentration.*

The Bible, according to 1 Corinthians 7:35 (NKJV), says "… and that you may serve the Lord without distraction."

As we are renewing our minds in Christ (covered in Chapters Seven and Eight), throughout our lives we will be faced with and/or challenged by distractions. However, it is how we relate to those distractions that can influence our journey. Please know that this is the case for everyone, regardless of one's station in life.

Not all distractions are bad. Some distractions are meant to cause you to either get on a path to God or to get *back* on a godly path. Because God already has in place whatever it takes for you to get on the right track.

For example, a good distraction presented in the Bible happened with Saul, whose name was later changed to Paul. Saul was on his way to killing more Christians. In Acts 9:4-8, Saul was journeying along a road from Jerusalem heading toward Damascus, "when suddenly a light shone around him from heaven …," and this was a godly distraction that caused him to talk with Jesus. By the story's end, Saul was converted; his name was changed to Paul, he spent the rest of his life serving God, and Paul became one of the greatest apostles. The apostle Paul went on to write between thirteen and fourteen books of the New Testament. All of this, I believe, began from the light of a godly distraction from heaven.

Let's talk about ungodly distractions. I'm talking about those distractions that work to delay or stop your life journey with God. Look at the example of King David and his infatuation with Bathsheba. According to 2 Samuel 11:2 (NKJV), it says, "… one evening that David arose from his bed and walked on the roof of the king's house. And from the roof he saw a woman bathing, and the woman was very beautiful to behold." Well, the details of this story, in a nutshell, is that Bathsheba was married to another man; and, sadly, Bathsheba conceived a child (2 Samuel 11:5) by King David. To cover up the misdeed, King David arranged to have her husband killed on the frontline of battle. I believe that all of this began when King David allowed himself to become distracted by Bathsheba's beauty. Understand that the distraction did not lie in Bathsheba's beauty, where she was or what she was doing; the distraction was the lust that King David allowed to enter into his thoughts. Remember, in the prior chapter, when we discussed how to cast down sinful, negative thoughts (2 Corinthians 10:5).

King David was an earthly king for God. He messed up, but God still used him. With all his faults, it is well-noted that he had a heart after God (1 Samuel 13:14 & Acts 13:22).

As you continue to read *In All Your Getting, Get Understanding!*, for whatever it is worth, hear my heart. Time is not waiting for anyone. There are things you want to do. There are places you want to visit. There are goals you want to achieve. There are also dreams that you want to become a reality. The godly desires of your heart are the desires that you want to see manifested. So pay attention, stay focused, and do not allow distractions, especially negative distractions, to hinder you or change your mind about what you believe God has said to you, i.e., the godly vision that He has shared with you. And know that when distractions come up, there will be questions. In many situations, I have asked myself, "What is this distraction really about?" And to get really real, in my talks with God, I may even put it this way, "Okay God, what's up with this?" What I am trying to do is to get at the origin, the root, of the distraction in my life. And this is serious because time is ticking. Not only do I want to identify the distraction, and understand what I am to learn from it, but also, I do not want to give in to any distractions that will get me off my path with God.

Ooo-wee! This brings us to a point regarding the ticking of time. If you read my devotional collection, titled *Any Day Devotion*, which is a Bible-based resource for daily living, as you explore these daily encouragements, you will discover another theme called *Tic-Toc Time Waits for No One!* This devotional read challenges you to think and gain understanding in real time, right now. It will also lead you to examine that which has been in your heart, and how to act on it. This is one way to prevent regrets about putting off what you know you should be doing for God, i.e., spending time with family, taking a vacation, going back to school, working a ministry in church, or seeing a doctor. The list can be endless, and if you put them off, the results can be catastrophic. Make sure you get this devotional!

Let's move on —

Let me ask you a few questions. If you begin to ponder on the answers, I believe that you will also begin to ignite tangible movement toward your accomplishments. In the 1975 film, titled, *Mahogany,* Diana Ross performed the film's signature song from its soundtrack. It was titled, *Do You Know Where You're Going To?* The first stanza of that song, written by Gerry Goffin and Michael Masser, offered some pivotal life questions. The lyrics ask if you're satisfied with your life. It goes on to ask, in so many words, if you have a plan for your life. Where are you going? The song even goes on to mention how the two star-crossed lovers in the film somehow let their dreams slip away — they let time tic-toc away before they even realized it. So take these as self-examinations and apply them to your life.

Have you reached, or are you still in hot pursue of your personal, professional and spiritual goals? Where are you in the progress of these areas of life, for which I believe, you have prayed? What do you need to do differently to see more progress — between now and the next few days, or the next coming weeks or months and/or even years?

The opposite of distraction is focus. You can stay focused by commanding your concentration to focus on your goal, not your distraction. Do understand that one's focus can become blurry, but do not lose heart, just know and accept that adjustments may need to happen. And only you can truly know that from within. Rely on the Holy Spirit to help you. Work to block out your distractions, especially, the ungodly ones. And please know that all this takes practice, but it is possible for us to learn to do.

This brings me to a point. Do you recall that in Chapter Seven, I mentioned the disciple, Peter, walking on water? He was doing fine until he took his eyes off of Jesus, which caused him to lose focus by looking at the boisterous wind (Matthew 14:30).

Whenever we take our eyes off God (i.e., not reading, studying, and meditating on the Word of God, etc.), it is possible for us to lose focus and to begin to sink via worry, envy, jealousy, and by harboring un-forgiveness in our hearts toward other people. However, what I love about the story is that Jesus came to Peter's rescue. Matthew 14:31 (NKJV) says, "And immediately Jesus stretched out His hand and caught him, and said to him, 'O you of little faith, why did you doubt?'"

Here's a jewel to help us based on Peter sinking in the water when he took his eyes off Jesus. I believe in the importance of this selected scripture because it will help us to maintain our focus on God. I provided three different translations:

- Hebrew 12: 2 (TLB), "Keep your eyes on Jesus, our leader and instructor."
- Hebrew 12:2 (Phillips), "… our eyes fixed on Jesus the source and the goal of our faith."
- Hebrew 12:2 (NKJV), "… looking unto Jesus, the author and finisher of our faith …"

Child of God, if we are not focused, then today, we must get focused on what matters most in our lives. Too much earthly time has been wasted thus far. So let's stay on the course with God by not allowing any distractions to stop or hinder our progress! God wants you and me to be aware of our distractions.

Check this out: One day, I was in my study room, reading and meditating on the Word of God. I was enjoying my quiet time with God. A time that is all-needed to rejuvenate my godly focus and effectiveness in ministry, and in life. Suddenly, I heard my granddaughter call out to my wife, and I heard my wife respond to her. The commotion jolted me out of my meditation. *Was my granddaughter hurt? Did she need something that only I could get for her?* Those were just some of the notions that took over my thoughts. I also knew, without a doubt, that if either of those notions were the case, my wife would have sought my assistance. Well, my wife responded to our granddaughter; she said something that did not involve me, and clearly, my assistance was not needed. But still, I involved myself by addressing what I had heard. All that was going on outside my study was a distraction, an innocent distraction. However, know that it was a distraction that I allowed. I had a choice in that moment not to let it detour me from my time with God.

Don't forget David and Bathsheba. I believe there are constant distractions on this journey of life that we, including me, can fall prey to before we even realize it. But by working to control our focus, on the good things of life, we can learn to recognize most distractions before they can cause harm. Distractions will never go completely away, but trust that the Holy Spirit will always be there to lead you through.

So, as you continue to read *In All Your Getting, Get Understanding!* let it help you to distinguish between engaging in productive and Kingdom work as opposed to engaging in busy work or emotional work. What you do for yourself, and for God also takes wisdom. And that's why it is so important to stay connected to the Holy Spirit's guidance. If you feel that you have lost focus toward any God-thing in your life, please see Jesus via the Word of God. He is stretching out His hands to help you just as He had done with Peter. He wants to help you in every area of your life. While doing that, let's have a made-up mind and refuse to be distracted, especially by unimportant things. Let's refuse to be distracted by nonsensical people, situations and time-stealers, trying to stop or delay what you need to do.

Child of God, God has great things for you and I. Stay on the course of what God has already designed for you. And take heed to what King David said to his son, Solomon, which we will discuss in the last chapter of this handbook. In Proverbs 4:7b (NKJV) it boldly states, "… In All Your Getting, Get Understanding!"

CHAPTER TEN — In All Your Getting, Get Understanding!

Attention! This is a Spiritual Self-examination Announcement: Pride will keep you from asking questions that will help you to *get understanding*. Now, back to our *Regular Christian Programming to Get Understanding.*

According to Proverbs 4:7 (NKJV) it says, "Wisdom is the principal thing; therefore get wisdom and in all your getting get understanding."

On www.dictionary.com, one can find a definition for these two words:

- *Wisdom* — the quality or state of being wise; knowledge of what is true or right coupled with just judgment as to action; sagacity, discernment, or insight.

- *Understanding* — mental process of a person who comprehends; comprehension; personal interpretation:

Since wisdom is the quality or state of being wise, then one should surmise that he or she should also seek a keen understanding of wisdom. By owning the understanding of the wisdom that the Holy Spirit puts in you, you will be able to activate that wisdom — for your good. With that said, also acknowledge that it is possible to have wisdom without a clear understanding of how to use it, or even worse, not activating it. It's possible to know better, but not to do better.

Having wisdom should reflect in your life. But what if you feel that you lack wisdom? Then follow what James 1:5 (NKJV) says, "If any of you lacks wisdom, let him ask of God, who gives to all liberally and without reproach, and it will be given to him." So there is no excuse for not having and/or seeking for wisdom. Get wisdom, and get an understanding of that wisdom, and intertwine one with the other.

Wisdom, and understanding the wisdom that has been set inside you should be so ingrained in you that it will shine in your conversations, in your actions, in your decisions, even in your heart's desires. Wisdom and understanding will own an ever-presence in your life. Let wisdom and understanding manifest in your life.

Listen: *This is a Spiritual Announcement:* This is not hocus pocus! These attributes come, and become stronger along the way of renewing your mind, and developing your personal relationship with Jesus Christ.

Back to our *Regular Christian Programming to Get Understanding*: Take your time when you are needing to make major decisions, but hurry up to get clear understanding of the situations with which you're being faced. Now, know that in some situations, an answer may manifest on the spot; while in other situations, answers may take some time. Because we are engaged, constantly, in conversations with God, by faith, the Holy Spirit has already started downloading the wisdom and understanding that we need in those situations.

Let's move on —

Check out these two selected verses:

Proverbs 18:2 (AMP) says, "A [closed-minded] fool does not delight in understanding,
But only in revealing his personal opinions [unwittingly displaying his self-indulgence and his stupidity]."

Although we do not have time for nonsensical people, as previously stated; and while in the midst, we are also being careful not to let them distract us, please be still — if only for a moment — to allow some godly discernment to seep in. Listen, and do not rush to judgment because this may be an opportunity to share God's Word. You may also possibly gain additional understanding for yourself. Accomplishing this takes growth in Christ.

Hearing God's voice through the scriptures, with the help of the Holy Spirit, will guide you when you are faced with these opportunities. Caution: beware of possessing puffed-up pride. Being excited about your newfound faith, you could run the risk of overwhelming others with what you've learned. Also, it may prevent your ability to remain humble enough to ask the questions that you need to ask.

For example, proud people tend to elevate themselves above others. Check this out: I spent many years serving in the United States Navy, staying longer than I should have at each level/pay grade. This was a disappointing fact because often those I supervised and taught routinely made the best of the knowledge I had to give them, and advanced to the next levels/pay grades beyond me. How was this happening? It was because I routinely allowed false pride to prevent me from seeking the full understanding and wisdom I needed to advance, myself. I was so intent on looking good in front of my superiors that I harbored in the mindset of neither asking for help nor inquiring about how to advance in my job field and pay grade. This was foolish, stupid — I'm talking about my actions and the way I was looking at things — and it was unbeneficial.

Looking back on this, I realize that my managers may have perceived my actions as my lack of initiative. Perhaps they thought that I did not want to advance. One of the reasons for this major misstep was my prideful mindset of knowing-it-all when I did not know. Considering this, take a look at Proverbs 16:18 (NKJV). It says, "Pride goes before destruction, and a haughty spirit before a fall." Wow!

Let's move on —

Be careful not to blindly close your mind to others or to what others may have to say. Do be mindful and respectful of others. And this premise runs across race, creed, class, and religion. And by the same token, remember that someone else's opinion is just that — their opinion. You have the choice and the free will to either accept or reject it. And if you do decide to make a move on what a person says or their expressed feelings, check it against the Word of God — trusting the Holy Spirit to help you.

Check this selected scripture:

Psalm 119:130 (NKJV) says, "The entrance of Your words gives light; it gives understanding to the simple."

God loves us; the Holy Spirit ensures that we are getting the understanding of whatever the matter is before us, at-hand. However, we cannot get it by being lazy. We have responsibility in this. Again, this is not hocus pocus. We need to invoke the compassion to know, and to press toward all that the Holy Spirit wants to download into our spirit. In addition, and this is exciting to me because I have personally experienced this, when the Holy Spirit downloads its wisdom and understanding of that wisdom, your path lights up. And when that happens, you will see far better, spiritually. All of this will benefit you from the spiritual into the natural.

One of the most important things for any believer to do, besides renewing their mind, during their time on this Earth, is to get understanding. Far too many believers, to include myself, have gotten into trouble due to preventable situations. These situations might not have happened if only they (and me) had gotten some biblical understanding, applied it. And let me make the point, one more time, that it is not enough to just get understanding, but also one needs to use that understanding. Sitting on knowledge, but not using it is just as detrimental.

One of the causes for not understanding and/or for ignoring understanding, I believe, is journeying in the negative thoughts of the mind. Seeking to renew one's mind in God gets rid of all the garbage that this world intends to use against us as a suffocating tool. Also, beware of allowing your mind, and actions, to be shaped/molded into just existing; and not taking it upon yourself to research to find the true purpose of all that comes your way. Isn't it true that you first read the instructions on a medicine bottle before taking the medication? Well, it's the same thing when it comes to asking the questions that can lead to getting the understanding of the things, people and situations that confront you.

I recall buying my BMW which has Run-Flat Tires. Run-Flat Tires are also known as tubeless tires. At the time, I didn't know much about tubeless tires. Okay, the truth of the matter is that it was the first time I had heard anything about a tubeless tire or the term, Run-Flat Tires. My wife and I, gleaming in the glow of the showroom, went blank when the car dealer asked, "Do you know anything about this car and these tires?"

Finally, my response was a resounding, prideful and emotional, “Yes.” And, men, you may understand this when I stress the fact that I was standing there in front of my wife.

Newsflash: Men, it’s okay to reveal that you may not know something in your wife’s presence. She is your helpmate. God has given you your wife to help you. Perhaps, she knows something that you do not know. And it is okay because the Bible says that, “For this reason a man shall leave his father and mother be joined to his wife, and the two shall become one flesh,” Ephesians 5:31 (NJKV).

Well, eleven months into driving our car, we fell victim to our first flat. I believe that’s when I received my first bit of understanding — our new BMW had not come with a spare tire. And here comes the lesson: Run-Flat Tires are designed to last for a fifty-mile stretch, and only while driving slow. We were on the highway, driving to the beach, sunroof-bathing, and all. It was a lovely day — until that flashing yellow tire light danced upon the dashboard.

I pulled over to inspect the tire, our BMW hobbled to the nearest gas station, and my second bit of newfound understanding came when the gas station attendant informed me that not only would my tire *not* take a patch, but also it was against the law to patch a Run-Flat Tire. Third, such a tire is something that has to be ordered.

Back in that beautiful car dealer's showroom, with my adoring wife by my side, intentionally not seeking or applying the wisdom and the understanding that I needed, proved to be a costly venture. I eventually paid nearly three times more than I had ever paid to replace a tire.

So be mindful of your emotions, and false pride, when embarking on anything. Wait to accrue wisdom and understanding from the Holy Spirit, and don't be afraid to ask questions. This is especially true, while we are growing up and becoming familiar with God's voice via scripture. Look what John 10:27 (NKJV) says, "My sheep [Christians] hear My voice, and I know them, and they follow Me."

Child of God, it is your responsibility to get understanding about being the son or daughter of God. So seek God and get understanding regarding your purpose. Constantly build up your relationship with God, your Heavenly Father. The Word of God will cause us all to walk together in unity (Psalm 133:1).

And don't forget, *In All Your Getting, Get Understanding!*

# # #

— Lasting Words from the Author

Child of God, thank you for spending time with me, and for reading *In All Your Getting, Get Understanding!* One of the most important things about living a life in Christ is that we should finish well. We want to hear our Lord, according to Matthew 25:23 (NKJV), say to each one of us, "… well done, good and faithful servant; you have been faithful over a few things."

Let us pray: Father, I thank you for this precious reader who invested in this *Handbook*, and who will prayerfully continue to seek You in every area of his or her life. I pray for this precious reader's dreams, goals and godly desires to come now — In Jesus' name!

Father, I thank you that we are more than a conqueror, and that no weapons formed against us shall prosper. In addition, whatever You have assigned and purposed this reader to do, I pray that he or she will move forward in that purpose. I pray that as stewards, he or she will move forward in faith, and receive abundant increases for Your glory. In Jesus' name, AMEN!

In All Your Getting, Get Understanding! is a handbook that intricately covers, what I believe, are four very important factors when it comes to learning how to enhance your walk with God. They are:(1) knowing and acknowledging that the Holy Spirit is there with you; (2) engaging in an active search to find a pastor connected to a Bible-based church; (3) setting your journey on the renewing of your mind; and (4) learning how to grow up in, and work with the measure of faith that God has dealt to you. Renewing your mind is a life journey for EVERY Christian until he or she is presently with the Lord.

Prayerfully, this *Handbook* has cleared up many misunderstandings when it comes to understanding the Word of God and activating its power in one's life as well as helping individuals to strengthen their personal relationship with our heavenly Father. Hopefully, this venture has cleared up *religious* misunderstandings, generations-old. Child of God, remember that lies disintegrate as soon as you and I know the truth — and the truth shall make us free (John 8:32)!

Be Blessed!

###

ABOUT THE AUTHOR

Pastor Dennis Scott has been an ordained pastor for nearly twenty years. Pastor Scott has served as a volunteer in Prison Ministry for ten years and counting. In 2016, he became the director of Prison Ministry, operating out of the *Spirit of Faith Christian Center* (SOFCC), in Temple Hills, Maryland. He preaches and teaches to men and women behind bars on a regular basis.

Pastor Scott is retired military. He served in the U.S. Navy for twenty-four years. Counting his time spent in the military, and working as a contractor for the Federal government, in the Information Technology field, he has a total of thirty-seven years under his belt. Currently, he is an Information Security Analyst / Engineer in the Washington, D.C. metropolitan area.

The author went on to achieve a goal that he had harbored for more than thirty years by graduating from the University of Maryland University College (UMUC) in May, 2016, and receiving his bachelor's degree in Information Cyber-security.

Pastor Scott, a native of New Jersey, makes his home in Maryland with his wife of thirty-three years, their three children and their one granddaughter.

For events, workshops, book signings and interviews, connect with Pastor Scott via the website www.3dennis7.com or send an email to 3dennis7@gmail.com .

Bible translations used:

Amplified Bible (AMP)

Good News Translation (GNT)

King James Version (KJV)

New American Standard Bible (NASB)

New Century Version (NCV)

New International Version (NIV)

New King James Version (NKJV)

New Living Translation (NLT)

Phillips New Testament (PHILLIPS)

###

Made in the USA
Middletown, DE
19 December 2017